Across the Curriculum

with Favorite Authors

Dr. Seuss

Written by John and Patty Carratello

Illustrated by Cheryl Buhler, Sue Fullman, and Keith Vasconcelles

The authors wish to thank Barbara Pelham for her valuable help.

Teacher Created Resources, Inc.
6421 Industry Way
Westminster, CA 92683
www.teachercreated.com

ISBN: 978-1-55734-450-2

©1992 Teacher Created Resources, Inc.
Reprinted, 2009
Made in U.S.A.

Table of Contents

Introduction

Our teaching is enriched daily by the wealth of outstanding authors who give us words and pictures to engage, motivate, and inspire our students. Through these authors, our students become acquainted with worlds and ideas beyond their own and emerge as more aware, active, and enthusiastic readers.

In this author series, one author is spotlighted in each resource book. Teachers and students have the opportunity to participate in an in-depth study of each author's work and style.

In this book you will find:

- Sample lesson plans

- Biographical information for a closer look at the author's life, style, motivations, and place in literary history

- Ways to design a classroom to generate interest in the author

- Cross-curricular lessons according to this format:
    - ✓ book summaries
    - ✓ *Before Reading the Book* ideas
    - ✓ *While Reading the Book* ideas
    - ✓ *After Reading the Book* ideas

- A culminating activity which will serve to showcase the students' involvement with the author

- Assessment tools structured to stimulate critical thinking skills

- A bibliography and answer key

We are confident the author approach to studying literature will be a satisfying experience for you and your students!

Sample Lesson Plans

These lessons are just a suggested guide. Use your judgment and your students' enthusiasm to guide your planning.

Preparation

- Preview the books and activities suggested in this resource.
- Collect the Dr. Seuss books you want to use in the author study. (pages 2 and 111)
- Create a classroom environment to stimulate an interest in Dr. Seuss. (page 9)

Lesson 1

- Present biographical information on Dr. Seuss. (page 7)
- Distribute Dr. Seuss' picture for a class art project. (page 6) You may suggest a number of ways students can use his picture. Here are just a few:

  - ☆ Color with crayons, chalk, or marker.
  - ☆ Paint with available painting materials.
  - ☆ Create a mosaic with tiny pieces of construction paper.
  - ☆ Trace on tracing paper and overlay it on a quote from one of his books.
  - ☆ Use as the background for a tissue paper collage.

- Discuss and demonstrate the writing and illustrating style that has brought Dr. Seuss much fame. (page 8)
- Give the students an opportunity to write and draw in his style. (page 8)

Lesson 2 through Lesson 14, an overview

- Present the "Before Reading the Book" activities you find most appropriate for your students and curriculum.
- Be sure to practice reading the book aloud before you present it to your students.
- During your class reading, monitor your students' ability to listen actively. Watch for physical clues, as well as questions, answers, and comments that are generated by active student involvement.
- Present appropriate "While Reading the Book" activities.
- Extend the book by encouraging "After Reading the Book" activities that are of interest to your students.

Sample Lesson Plans

Lesson 2, an elaboration *And To Think That I Saw It On Mulberry Street*

- Present any number of "Before Reading the Book" activities for *And To Think That I Saw It On Mulberry Street*. This book is particularly good to use for instilling the importance of imagination.

- While reading the book, speculate on what Marco will "see" next. Distinguish between reality and fantasy. Predict what Marco might have "seen" next if he hadn't reached home.

- After reading the book, draw pictures, write stories, and play games involving the use of a vivid imagination! (page 10)

Lesson 15

- Prepare students for the Culminating Activity on pages 98 to 104.

- Review Dr. Seuss books you have studied.

- Share ideas for "Mulberry Street." (page 98)

- Prepare "Mulberry Street." (pages 99 to 104)

- Choose designs. Many are provided in this resource book.

- Write rhymes about sights that are seen on "Mulberry Street."

- Write book reviews about Dr. Seuss books to be "mailed" in the "Mulberry Street" mailbox. (page 98)

- Invite another class to your "Mulberry Street."

Lesson 16

- Choose the assessments that are appropriate for your students' interest and ability level.

- When conducting the application assessment suggested on page 107, you may find that it can be extended into a week's lesson. Students usually take great interest and pride in developing their own lessons for the study of a book.

- If this is successful, encourage them to develop lessons for other Dr. Seuss books working in small groups. The entire class can then enjoy many more books by the author, and the students have personalized their learning!

Lesson 17

Visit the library. Encourage students to read more books written and illustrated by Dr. Seuss. (page 111)

Dr. Seuss

About the Author

Theodor Seuss Geisel was born on March 2, 1904 in Springfield, Massachusetts to Theodore Robert and Henrietta (Seuss) Geisel. From a very early age, his father taught him the importance of seeking perfection. Throughout his 54 year writing career, Ted Geisel kept perfection his goal, and attained it as a writer and as an educator.

Along the way, Ted Geisel could have been daunted from the career that brought him so much fame and respect. His high school art teacher told him that he would never learn how to draw. Members of his college fraternity voted him the least likely to succeed. But, while drawing a flying cow during a college lecture, a woman named Helen Palmer complimented Ted's drawing, and encouraged him to pursue an art career. They married in 1927, and she continued to help support, inspire, and work with him until her death in 1967.

During the early years of the Geisel marriage, Ted earned money by creating advertising art and cartoons for magazines, newspapers, and billboards. "Quick, Henry! The Flit!" was an ad campaign he created to sell a spray insecticide, and this ad contract helped him earn a living during the tough financial times of the Depression.

During the 1930s, school-age children were limited to simplistic "Dick and Jane" books. Ted Geisel's first attempt to write an imaginative children's book met with rejection after rejection. The publishers insisted it wouldn't sell because there was nothing on the market like it. However, one company decided to give *And To Think That I Saw It On Mulberry Street* a chance, and the book was an immediate success. It seemed as if children and their parents were ready for a change! It was with this book that he introduced his pseudonym, Dr. Seuss.

Here is his own explanation of this name, as quoted from "The Miracle of Dr. Seuss" by Cynthia Lindsay, *Good Housekeeping*, December, 1960.

"The 'Dr. Seuss' name is a combination of my middle name and the fact that I had been studying for my doctorate when I quit to become a cartoonist. My father had always wanted to see a Dr. in front of my name, so I attached it. I figured by doing that, I saved him about ten thousand dollars. "

In 1956, his old college presented him with an honorary doctorate degree, making the Dr. of Dr. Seuss official!

Book after book followed for Dr. Seuss. His books were easy to read, friendly, and imaginative, and young readers opened them enthusiastically. In 1957, he entered a new phase of his writing with *The Cat in the Hat*. This book marked the start of Beginner Books, a company dedicated to the creation of books written with a limited, simple vocabulary that still have a content that motivates children to read. This venture, a division of Random House, filled a much-needed gap in early reading education. Ted Geisel, who had long-wanted to be a writer and an educator, had realized his dream.

The career of Ted Geisel was filled with books, documentaries, television specials, movies, and awards. But his success did not come easily. He worked hard to make his books just right.

"Writing books for children is hard work, a lot harder than most people realize. And it never gets easier. The most important thing about me is that I work slavishly -write, rewrite, reject, and polish incessantly ...

I am trying to capture an audience. Most every child learning to read has problems, and I am just saying to them that reading is fun.

As quoted in Books Are by People *by Lee Bennett Hopkins, Citation Press, 1969*

For those of us who have read and enjoyed the books of Theodor Seuss Geisel, his reading is fun!

The Style of Dr. Seuss

In the nearly 50 books Dr. Seuss has written and illustrated, there is a style that is easily recognizable. His drawings are free-style, clear, simple, and colorful. His writing is clear and simple, too, full of humor and cleverness. His stories are imaginative, fun, and compassionate. If there is a moral in one of his stories, it often develops so naturally from the plot, readers recognize the message easily and eagerly.

Draw a Dr. Seuss character. Add details that would be true to his style.

Write your own story using some or all of the words Dr. Seuss used in his first limited vocabulary story, *The Cat in the Hat.*

the	and	him	of	lots	ship	when	shake	way
sun	said	step	will	game	some	make	had	they
did	how	on	show	call	milk	get	their	any
not	wish	mat	then	up	dish	be	them	her
shine	had	cat	your	put	hop	but	pat	home
it	hat	mind	down	oh	saw	tame	something	hear
was	do	he	if	knew	ran	give	find	mother
too	go	why	what	fall	these	fast	come	near
wet	out	you	say	hold	rake	fox	fly	think
to	ball	sit	our	high	man	back	kites	rid
play	know	for	as	tail	got	hit	after	nothing
so	at	is	but	stand	red	box	hall	net
we	could	sun	fish	book	fan	big	wall	bet
sat	like	no	one	fell	wood	thump	yet	sunny
in	one	can	away	hand	head	shut	string	plop
house	little	have	tell	cup	came	hook	gown	last
all	bit	fun	want	my	from	take	dots	stop
that	bump	funny	should	look	things	top	pink	pack
cold	some	here	me	into	tip	white	playthings	dear
day	went	good	about	cake	pot	his	bed	shame
I	made	games	this	top	lit	bow	those	shut
there	us	new	now	hold	sank	pick	jumps	sad
with	jump	tricks	fear	two	deep	see	kicks	kind
Sally	looked	a	are	books	shook	bite	hops	yes
two	another	lot	bad	toy	bent	would	kinds	mess
tall	always	who	thing	picked	let	asked	how	she

Setting Up for Dr. Seuss

Students will be eager to learn about Dr. Seuss and his work in a classroom that is bright and lively with his books, art, and rhyme.

Be sure that you have allowed plenty of room for the display of Dr. Seuss projects. A large bulletin board area would provide an excellent showcase. A wire strung across the classroom can serve as a place to clip up drying artwork as well as a display area for finished work. Projects can also hang from strings on the ceiling. You can even display a project a day on your desk or podium!

A center for storage of art supplies where children can easily reach materials will make setting up for various projects easier. Here are some ideas:

- a basket for writing paper

- sentence or word strips

- pocket chart for sentence or word strips

- a tub or box for smocks or paintshirts

- a supply of different sizes of paper on a low shelf

- a box for tissue paper scraps

- a tall plastic container for brushes that can be filled with water so brushes can be soaked before rinsing

- plastic margarine tubs for starch or glue mixtures (One for every two students works well).

- containers of pencils, pens, markers, and crayons

- a basket for scissors

- newspapers

- a roll of paper towels

- wipe cloths from the "rag bag"

- sponges for cleanup

And To Think That I Saw It On Mulberry Street

by Dr. Seuss
(Available in U.S. and Canada from Random House, 1937)

Summary

Marco's dad always tells his son to keep his eyes open on the way home from school, to see what he can see. Marco follows his father's advice as he walks homeward on Mulberry Street. However, the horse and wagon that he does see is not quite enough for Marco. He imagines a colorful and unusual parade of sights and sounds, returning home quite exhilarated! What he chooses to tell his father about his adventure will create quite an impact on the reader.

Before Reading the Book

- Determine a list of things you might see on a typical street in your city or town. (page 11) *And To Think I Saw It On Mulberry Street* was published in 1937. What do you think you might have seen on a typical street in 1937?

- Take a class walk down a street in your city or town. Ask students to record what they observe. (page 12)

- Ask your students if they have ever stretched the truth to make up good stories. Invite them to share their fascinating fabrications!

While Reading the Book

- Before turning each page, see if students can guess what kinds of changes Marco will make next.

- Choose your favorite imaginative picture and tell why it is your favorite.

- Turn to the page that ends "No time for more, I'm almost home." If Marco had time for more imagining, what do you think his next picture would have been? Draw and share it.

After Reading the Book

- Discuss Marco's father's opinion of his son's ability to clearly report information. (page 13)

- Talk about how much you like to share what you do and see with one or both of your parents.

- Why do you think Marco did not tell his father what he so vividly imagined?

- Retell the entire story from the father's point of view.

- What would the story have been like if you told it?

- Use your imagination to change the "observations" on page 14 to "fantasies."

- Make your own *And To Think I Saw It On Mulberry Street* book. (page 15)

What's on a Street?

Color the things on this page that you might see while walking down a street on your way home from school.

On the back of this paper, draw a picture of one more thing you might see on a street near where you live.

Observation Walk

Walk along a street in your city or town with your class. Keep a record of what you observe on your outing.

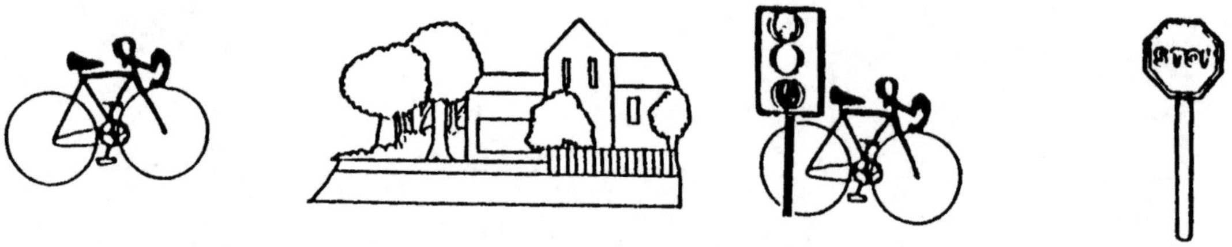

What I saw: _____

_____

_____

What I heard:_____

_____

_____

What I smelled: _____

_____

_____

What I touched: _____

_____

_____

What I thought about what I observed: _____

_____

_____

_____

Minnows into Whales

Marco's father tells his son to keep his eyes open as he walks home.

"But when I tell him where I've been
And what I think I've seen,
He looks at me and sternly says,
'Your eyesight's much too keen.

Stop telling such outlandish tales.
Stop turning minnows into whales.'"

What do you think his father means? Color these pictures and cut them out. Arrange them in a sequence that shows how Marco might turn "minnows into whales."

Observations into Fantasies

Use your imagination to change these "observations" into "fantasies."

observation	**fantasy**
observation	**fantasy**
observation	**fantasy**

And To Think . . .

Remember one of the observations you made on the class walk. Try to turn it into your own story like *And To Think I Saw It On Mulberry Street*. Use this page as a cover for your own story or design one of your own.

And to Think That I Saw It On

_____

by

_____

The Cat in the Hat

by Dr. Seuss
(Available in U.S. and Canada from Random House, 1957)

Summary

On a dreary, rainy day, Sally and her brother are at home alone with nothing to do when an uninvited visitor arrives with ideas for play that put the house in chaos. When the children see the mess, they fear it will never be clean by the time their mother returns. However, the Cat in the Hat cleans up with style, and just in time!

Before Reading the Book

- Brainstorm ideas for rainy day activities. (page 17)

- As a homework assignment, ask children to discuss with their parents specific rules they have at home when they are alone, or a parent is unable to come to the phone or door. Are friends allowed in? How should the phone be answered? What happens if someone knocks at the door? What are the steps to take in an emergency? The next day, discuss "home" rules as a class.

- Invite a police officer to visit the class to discuss what children should do if an emergency arises without an adult available, and ways to avoid dangerous situations.

- Ask children to think of several situations that could cause problems if they were home alone or a parent was unavailable. Record their ideas on separate cards or strips of paper. Divide the class into small groups and give each group one or two problems to discuss. Invite them to think of ways to respond to the problems and present their ideas to the class by role playing.

While Reading the Book

- Guide the reading of the story with questions such as these:

  — Have you ever been home on a rainy day with nothing to do? What would you do?

  — How do you think the children in this story were feeling? How would you feel?

  — Would the story be different if the Cat in the Hat told it? Rewrite some of it from the Cat's point of view.

- Count and list the objects that the cat can keep balanced in the air before everything falls.

- Have children make finger puppets (or stick puppets) to use as they retell the story. (page 18)

After Reading the Book

- Give students practice in matching rhyming words in rhyming games and activities. (page 19) The object of one game you can play is to make pairs of word cards that rhyme. You can also ask students to choose a card and write a word that rhymes with it on the board. Every rhyming pair is a point.

- Ask students to find places for all the items that the Cat in the Hat has left strewn about. (page 20)

- Ask students to draw a machine that would clean up their rooms. (page 21)

Rainy Day Ideas

Sally and her brother had "nothing to do" on a wet, rainy day. On the other hand, the Cat in the Hat was full of rainy day ideas!

What are some of the things you like to do on a rainy day? Write your ideas in the umbrella shapes below. Be sure that the ideas you choose are acceptable ones. Remember, you do not have the Cat in the Hat's marvelous machine to clean up after you! When you have finished, cut the umbrellas out and attach them to a "rain-covered" bulletin board.

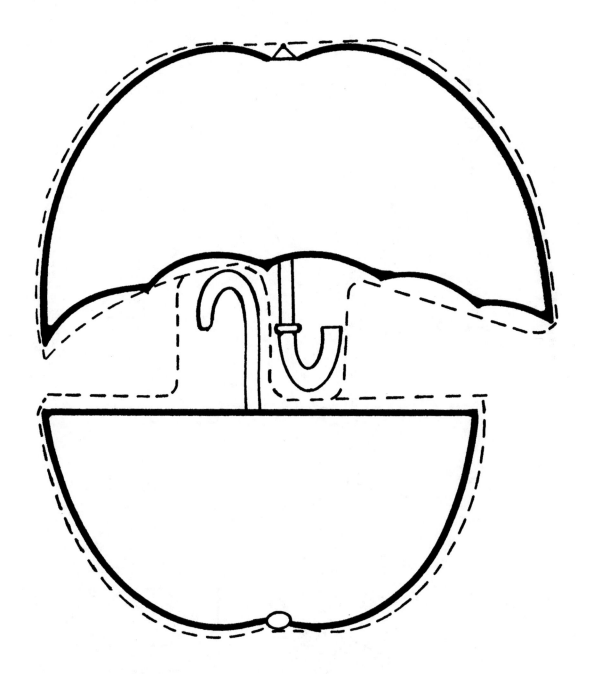

Draw a picture of you doing one of your ideas on a separate sheet of paper. Share your picture with the class.

Puppet Show!

These patterns may be duplicated on construction paper for finger puppets or enlarged and used with cardboard strips for stick puppets.

Complete the faces of these characters from *The Cat in the Hat*. Color and cut them out. Use glue to attach each face to a finger band made from a ½" x 3" (1.3 cm x 7.5 cm) strip of paper. Adjust the band to fit your finger and tape or glue it in place. Use these puppets to retell all or part of the story.

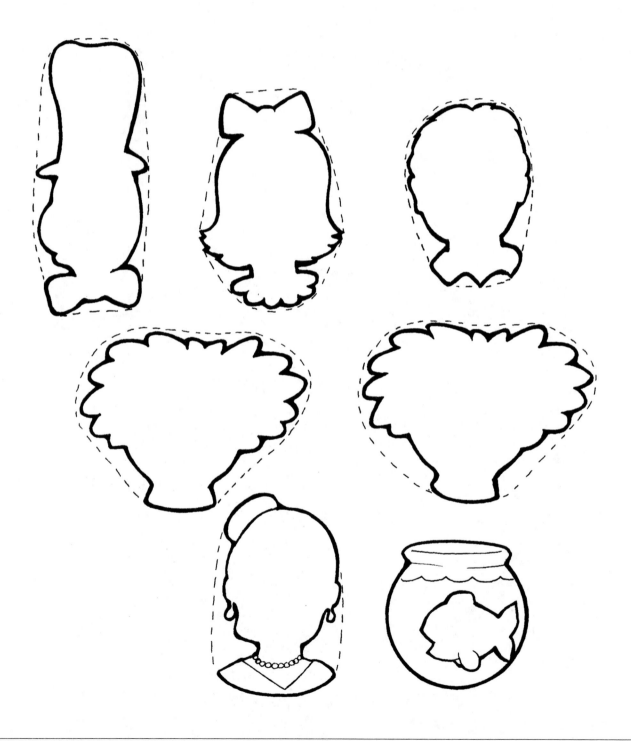

Rhyme Time!

Use these rhyming words to play rhyming games and build rhyming stories. You can match them; cut them out, attach to 3" x 5" (8 cm x 13 cm) cards, shuffle, and deal them; or attach them to rhyming artwork!

call	fall	ball	hall	wish
hat	that	cat	Pat	dish
sun	fun	cake	rake	cup
lit	bit	bump	thump	up
sunny	funny	gown	down	pot
say	day	play	away	not
stop	plop	now	how	make
tame	game	box	fox	shake
stand	hand	near	dear	string
hook	book	yes	mess	thing

What a Mess!

It looks like the Cat in the Hat has been here! Help clean up this room. Draw a line from something that is in the wrong place to where it could go. Color the picture.

The Marvelous Room Cleaning Machine!

Do you ever wish that you had an automatic room cleaning machine like the Cat in the Hat? How would it work? What would it look like? Invent a machine to clean your room and draw it here.

My room cleaning machine is called

_____

by _____

Yertle the Turtle and Other Stories

by Dr. Seuss
(Available in U.S. and Canada from Random House, 1958)

Summary

The turtles on the island of Sala-ma-Sond led a happy, contented life. Their pond provided everything they needed. However, their ruler, a turtle named Yertle, was not content to be master only of what he saw from his rock in the pond. He wanted to rule from a higher place, to be master of all he saw. He ordered turtles to climb upon each other to add height to his throne. But, Yertle was not satisfied and commanded his subjects pile on one another in greater numbers, at the expense of their own comfort. He was quite selfish. But soon, he found he could not be so demanding of his followers. Thanks to the effort of one very plain turtle, Yertle finally got what he deserved.

Before Reading the Book

- Over a few days or a few recess periods, play "Follow the Leader." Be sure everyone gets to be the leader for a short time.

- The next day for a ten minute period of time, allow only one person in the class to be leader. Ask for a volunteer with high self-esteem. Complete the activity on page 23.

- Discuss the qualities good leaders have.

While Reading the Book

- Make a turtle stack. (pages 24 and 25)

- Learn more about turtles. (page 26)

- Discuss Yertle's demands and Mack's reactions.

- Determine the meaning of the last sentence of the book. Apply its lesson to the past, present, and future.

After Reading the Book

- Predict the future of Yertle and the other turtles in the pond on the Island of Salama-Sond.

- Study democracy and slavery. *Yertle the Turtle* could be effectively taught during the month of January or February because of the work Martin Luther King, Jr. and Abraham Lincoln did to advance equal rights. (page 27)

- Read and discuss other turtle books such as *Franklin in the Dark* by Paulette Bourgeois (Kids Can Press, 1986) or *Turtle Tale* by Frank Asch (Dial, 1978).

Is It Fair?

Over the last few days at recess time, you have watched everyone in your class have the chance to be a leader.

What did you do when you were the leader?

_____

What are some of the things other people led that you enjoyed?

_____

_____

_____

If you could choose someone to be a leader for recess tomorrow, who would you choose?

_____

Why? _____

_____

_____

Do you like to play games where the same person always tells everyone else what to do? Why?

_____

_____

Would you like to have just one person be the leader every day for the rest of the school year? Why?

_____

_____

Do you like to be the leader? Why?

_____

_____

_____

Turtle Stack!

Using the materials listed below, make a turtle. When you are finished, join with your classmates to stack Yertle's throne. Work cooperatively to make the stack as high as you possibly can. Designate one of the turtles to be Yertle if you wish!

Materials Needed:

two lightweight paper plates

turtle patterns (page 25)

marking pens, crayons, colored pencils

stapler

Directions:

1. Color and cut out the turtle parts on page 25.

2. Make the carapace (top part of shell) and the plastron (bottom part of shell) from two paper plates. Be sure to draw the divisions of the turtle's shell. Color the shell as realistically as possible.

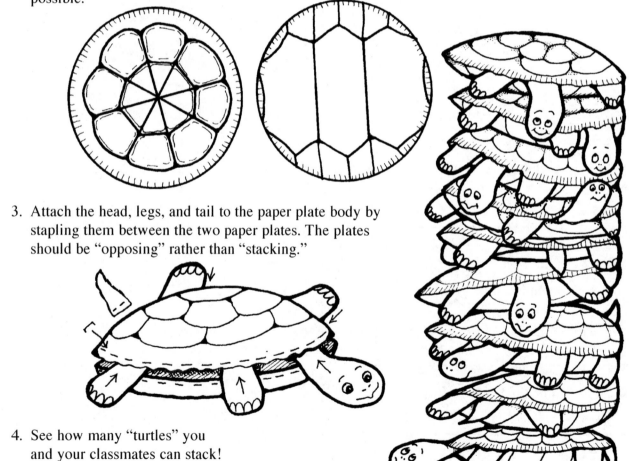

3. Attach the head, legs, and tail to the paper plate body by stapling them between the two paper plates. The plates should be "opposing" rather than "stacking."

4. See how many "turtles" you and your classmates can stack!

Turtle Stack!

Color and cut out the turtle head, legs, and tail on this page. Then follow the directions on page 24 to make a stacking turtle.

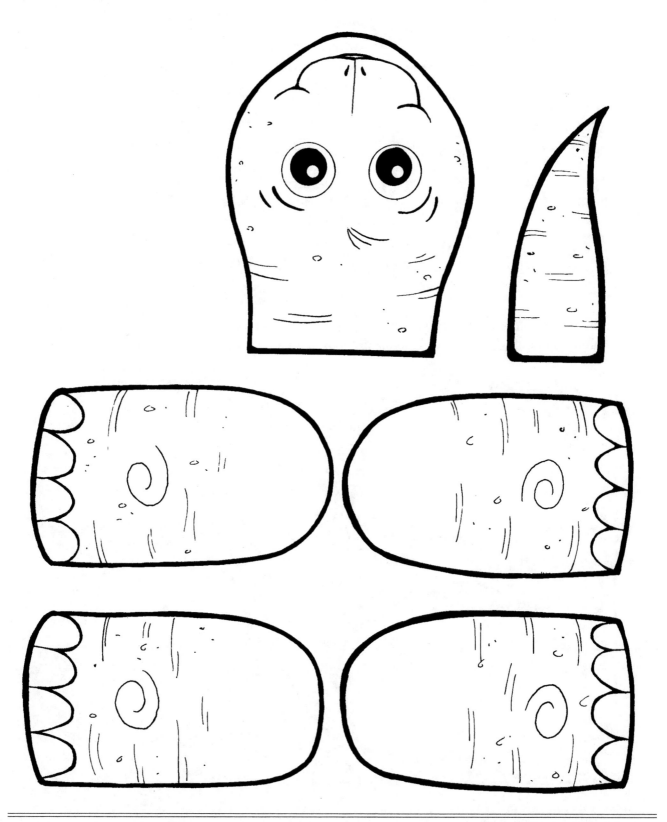

A Closer Look

Turtles are fascinating creatures. Here are just a few turtle facts you may find interesting.

Turtles first appeared on Earth about 200 million years ago, during the time of the dinosaurs.

Some turtles can live to be 100 years old.

A turtle has no teeth.

A turtle can feel pressure through its shell in the same way you can feel pressure if you press on your fingernail.

Find out more about turtles. Print some interesting facts you discover in the turtle shapes below. Cut out your turtle facts and add them to a bulletin board display.

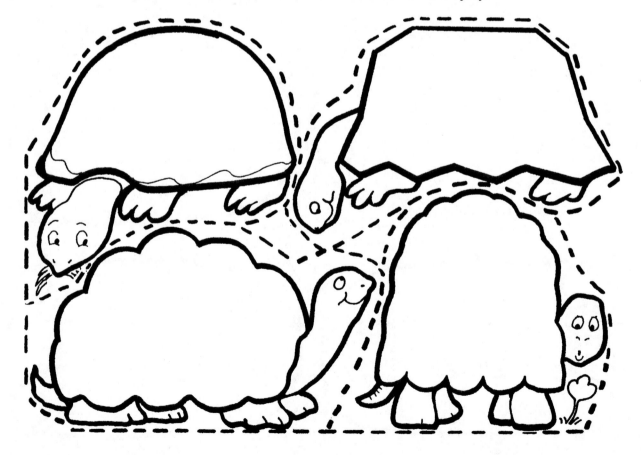

Democracy and Slavery

Yertle made demands upon the turtles of the pond that were quite selfish. Without regard to their pain or hunger, he expected them to obey his wishes without question. He did not seem to understand that all turtles in the pond had a right to be free to make their own choices.

In a democracy, all people (or turtles) have the right to be heard. The "plainest" person, just like Mack, can share his or her ideas and questions.

Do you think Yertle would have had success at building the throne of turtles if he had asked his followers if they wanted to do it? Why? _____

_____

_____

Do you think the turtles might have felt like Yertle's slaves?

Throughout history, people have been enslaved by others. What do you think it would be like to be someone's slave? Try it for a period of time at school today. Here's how:

- Your teacher will choose partners for everyone in the class. If there is an uneven number, one master will have two slaves.

- With the teacher's help, the masters will think of safe and appropriate things for the slaves to do, such as sharpening pencils, carrying books, hopping to lunch on one foot, and feeding a master raisins one by one.

- For a certain period of time, the slave will do everything the master tells him or her to do. Remind 'masters that their demands must be appropriate!

- At the end of the period of slavery, discuss your feelings. Also realize that for you, slavery was just a game. For those caught in the unjustness of real slavery, it is not a game.

- Change the master/slave relationship on the next day.

Throughout history, people have fought the injustice of slavery. What names come to your mind? Brainstorm a list of those who have fought for equal rights for others. Research the lives of these men and women and share what you have learned with the class.

Dr. Seuss adds his name to those fighting for equality with his gentle rhyme.

> *"And today the great Yertle, that Marvelous he,*
> *Is King of the Mud. That is all he can see.*
> *And the turtles, of course…all the turtles are free*
> *As turtles and, maybe, all creatures should be."*

The Foot Book

by Dr. Seuss
(Available in U.S. and Canada from Random House, 1968)

Summary

In this easy to read Beginner Book, we see a variety of feet, and perhaps understand our uniqueness just a bit more.

Before Reading the Book

- Spread a large piece of butcher paper on a concrete area near your classroom. Ask your students to take off their shoes and trace their left and right feet, making clear footprints. Ask students to sign their names by their prints. They can then cut a circle around their own prints, return to the classroom, and decorate their footprints with paint, tissue paper collage, fabric scraps, or other art materials.

- Ask each student to take off a shoe and place it in the center of a class circle. Discuss the variety of styles and sizes in the class shoe pile.

While Reading the Book

- Count the total number of feet pictures in *The Foot Book.*

- Use sets of feet to practice skip counting. (page 30)

- Count feet. (page 31)

- Match feet. (page 32)

- Label left and right feet. (page 29)

After Reading the Book

- Determine patterns based on types of feet or shoes. (page 33)

- Design unusual feet and/or shoes. Display your creations on a class Foot Board.

- Stage a footwear fashion show. Try to arrange for everyone in the class to wear a different type of shoe for the fashion show.

- Read a book about feet and shoes, such as *Whose Shoes Are These?* by Ron Roy and Rosemarie Hausherr (Clarion, 1988). This book also explains the origins and uses of various types of shoes. Students will find shoe history fascinating!

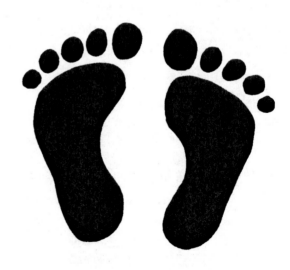

Left or Right?

Label these feet left or right. Color.

Count By. . .

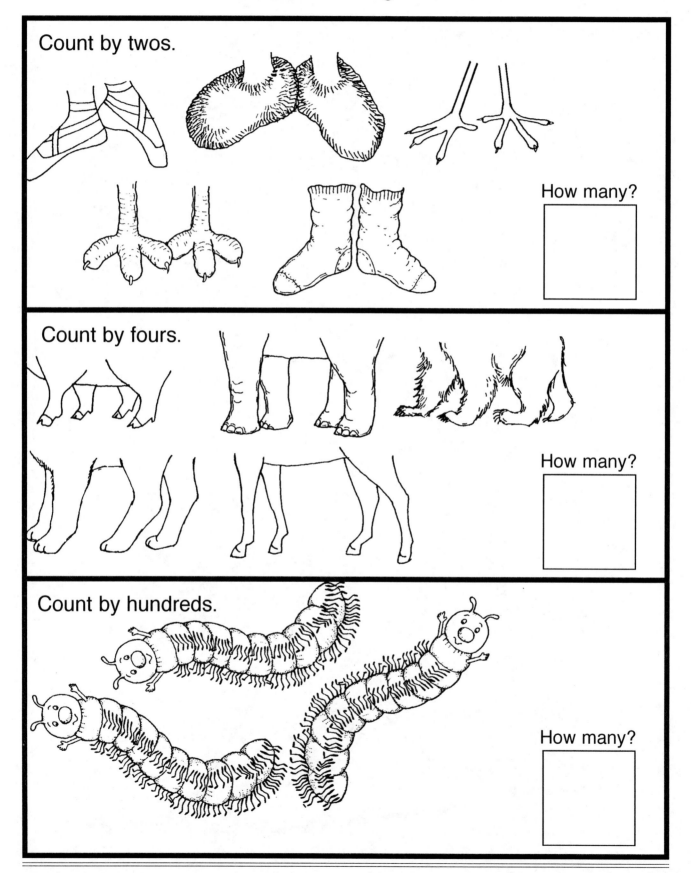

Count by twos.

How many?

Count by fours.

How many?

Count by hundreds.

How many?

Counting Feet

Feet at School

The following questions are about the feet that are in your classroom today.

1. How many feet are in your classroom? _ _ _____
2. How many girls' feet are in your classroom? _____
3. How many boys' feet are in your classroom? _____
4. How many feet are wearing tennis shoes? _____
5. How many feet are wearing sandals? _____
6. How many feet have white socks? _____
7. How many feet are not wearing socks? _____
8. How many feet can jump over two boxes? _____
9. How many feet are ticklish? _____
10. How many feet like to go barefoot _____

Feet at Home

The following questions are about the feet that are in your home today.

1. How many people feet live in your house? _____
2. How many feet are children's feet? _____
3. How many animal feet are in your house? (Do not count people feet in this count.) _____

Draw your own animal with as many feet as you want it to have.

Matching Feet

Color the feet that match with the same colors.

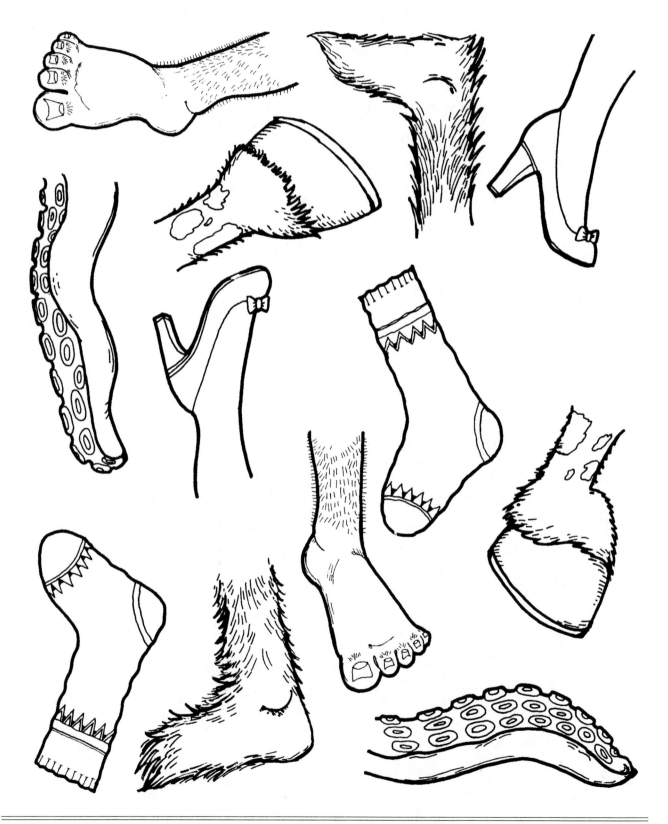

What's the Pattern?

Cut out the feet in the last row. Complete the pattern by pasting the correct foot to show what will come next.

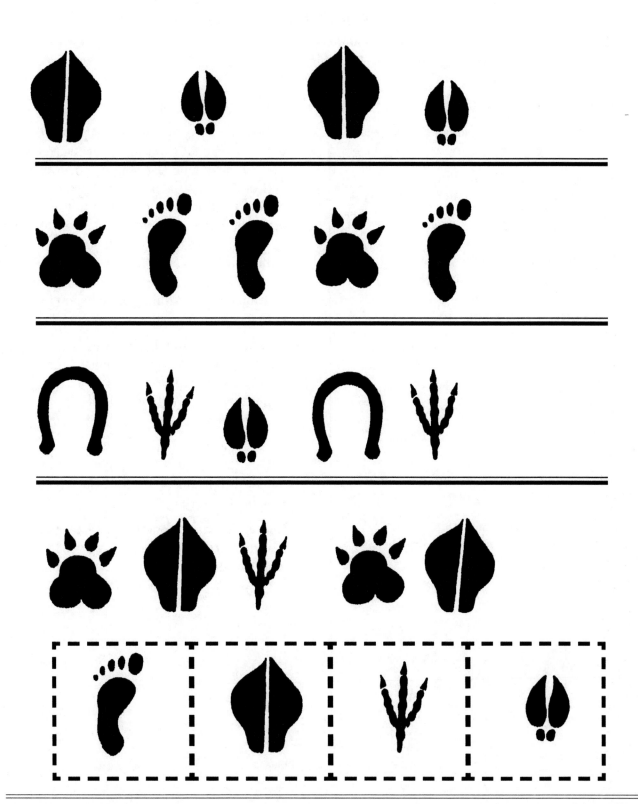

Dr. Seuss's A B C

by Dr. Seuss
(Available in U.S. and Canada from Random House, 1963)

Summary

Dr. Seuss takes beginning readers through the alphabet in alliterative fashion with the emphasis on FUN! Both capital and lower case letters are included.

Before Reading the Book

- Preview a variety of alphabet books for use in your center. (page 111)

- Set up an Alphabet Center in your classroom. You can surround children with a wealth of alphabet books and activities. (page 35)

- Brainstorm lists of things that begin with the twenty-six letters of the alphabet.

While Reading the Book

- Make up stories to go with each of the pictures.

- Compile lists of the words Dr. Seuss has used to illustrate each letter of the alphabet.

- Color capital and lower case letters. (pages 36, 37, and 38)

- Practice matching capital and lower case letters. (pages 36, 37, and 38)

- Practice sequencing the letters of the alphabet with connect-the-dot alphabet puzzles. (page 39)

After Reading the Book

- Divide the class in half. Give half of the class one capital letter in alphabetical order until all have letters. Then, give the other half of the class one lower case letter in alphabetical order. Direct them to find their alphabet partners. Each pair must try to think of as many things as possible that begin with their letter. They may write the words or draw pictures. When they have finished, distribute the remaining capital and lower case letters in the same way.

- Ask them to continue their partner brainstorming. They can "publish" their word ideas on strips to be used at the Alphabet Center for a word-to-letter matching activity.

- Encourage students to make their own alliterative alphabet books like those of Dr. Seuss, Kathleen and Michael Hague, and Graeme Base. (page 111)

- Cut out the capital and lower case letters that have been colored. Students may use these letters when they create their own alphabet books!

Alphabet Center

There is a glorious wealth of books that can be used to teach and reinforce alphabet skills in an enjoyable way. You may wish to develop an Alphabet Center in your classroom that will showcase these outstanding books as well as provide a place to display other alphabet-related materials.

Here are some ideas for activities that can be done at your center.

Capitals and Lower Case Letters

Use the capital and lower case letters on pages 36, 37, and 38 to:

1. Alphabetize upper and lower case letters.
2. Match capitals with their lower case partners.
3. Decorate covers or begin the pages of students' own alphabetical books.
4. Play a two-to-four person card game modeled after "Go Fish."
   - The object of the game is to match capital and lower case letters in pairs.
   - All players are dealt four cards. Any "instant" matches are placed in front of the player with the match.
   - Player #1 asks another player if he or she has the match for a card held. "Do you have a capital H?" If the player who is asked has it, he or she gives it to Player #1 who continues. If the player asked does not have the card Player #1 seeks, Player #1 draws from the pile. If he or she happens to draw the desired card, Player #1 continues the asking. If not, the turn belongs to Player #2.
   - This continues until all cards are matched. The player with the most matches wins.

Capitals and Lower Case Letters

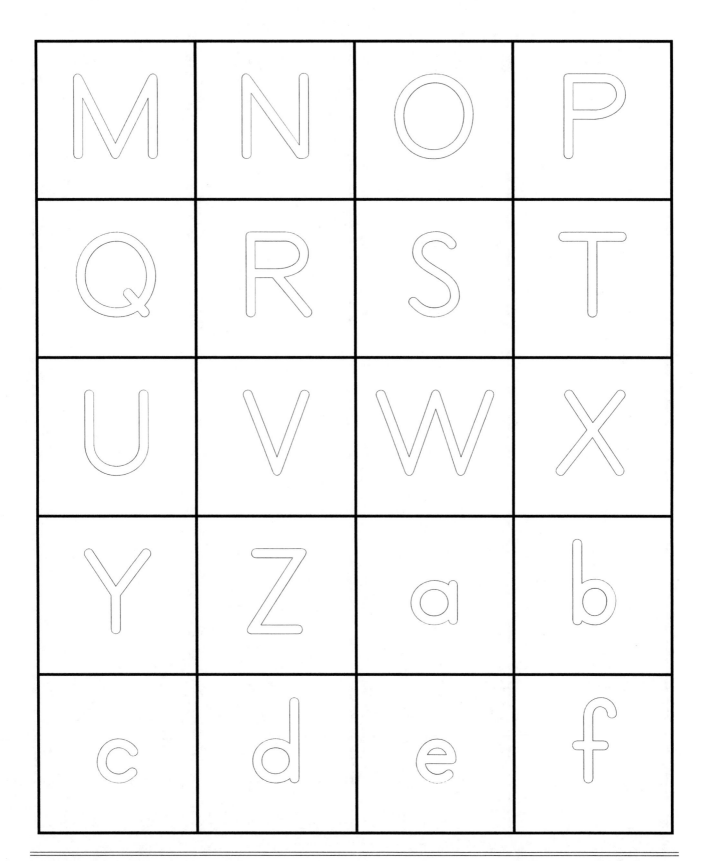

Capitals and Lower Case Letters

g	h	i	j
k	l	m	n
o	p	q	r
s	t	u	v
w	x	y	z

Alphabet Dot-to-Dot

Connect these letters in alphabetical order to discover the picture.

The King's Stilts

by Dr. Seuss
(Available in U.S. and Canada from Random House, 1939)

Summary

King Birtram was a hard working king, concerned about the safety and welfare of his kingdom. He devoted his days to maintaining the heavy, knotted roots of the Dike Trees that protected the island Kingdom of Dinn from being flooded by the water of the sea that surrounded it. After a hard day's work; King Birtram raced about the kingdom on his bright red stilts. The townsfolk loved their hard-working king, and delighted in his youth play. However, one man did not like the King's "foolish" play. In The King's Stilts, *readers discover what happened in the Kingdom of Dinn when the King's stilts were stolen.*

Before Reading the Book

- Ask students to design the perfect kingdom for a king and his followers.

- Discuss the types of things that could threaten a kingdom's safety.

- Invite students to share what their parents do for work and play.

- Brainstorm lists of things students like to do for fun. Rank them in order of class preference.

- Give a geography pre-test. (page 41)

While Reading the Book

- Using available art materials, make Dike Trees and Nizzards.

- Learn geographical ideas that are presented in *The King's Stilts*. Extend your knowledge of geography. (pages 42, 43, and 44)

- Discuss the main characters in the story in terms of causing and resolving conflicts.

- Draw what the Kingdom of Binn would have looked like if the King remained "stilt-less."

After Reading the Book

- Ask students to choose one of the characters in the story and write a journal entry as if they were that character. They can choose a Nizzard, a Patrol Cat, King Birtram, Eric, Lord Droon, or any other character!

- Give a geography post-test. (page 41)

- Make simple stilts and practice walking with them. (page 45)

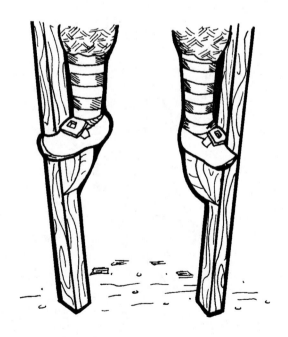

Geography Words

Look at the landforms drawn on this page. Use the words in the box to correctly label as many landforms as you know.

lake	**sea**	**valley**	**river**
island	**mountain**	**beach**	**peninsula**

Geography Lesson

In *The King's Stilts*, the Kingdom of Binn is a valley on an island in the middle of a sea. Do you know what a valley, an island, and a sea are? Valleys, islands, and seas are part of the land and water forms that make up our world. About 30% of the world's surface is land. About 70% of the world's surface is water.

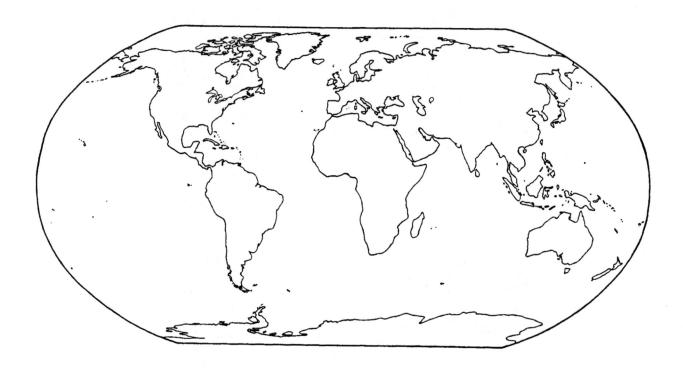

The world's land is made up of continents. The seven continents in order from largest to smallest are:

    1) Asia   3) North America   5) Antarctica   7) Australia

    2) Africa   4) South America   6) Europe

The world's water is made up of water forms such as oceans, seas, gulfs, lakes, and rivers.

The four largest bodies of water in order from largest to smallest are:

    1) Pacific Ocean   3) Indian Ocean

    2) Atlantic Ocean   4) Arctic Ocean

Use resources to help you label the continents and oceans on the map on this page.

Geography Lesson

The Kingdom of Binn was a valley on an island, surrounded by an unusual "wall" created by the roots of Dike Trees. Without the protection of the root system, the Kingdom of Binn would be covered by sea water.

A *valley* is a large "dip" or depression in the earth's surface. It is usually found to be surrounded by hills or mountains. In the case of the Kingdom of Binn, the valley is a dip in the land surrounded by a wall of Dike Trees.

An *island* is a piece of land that is completely surrounded by water. An island is smaller than a continent.

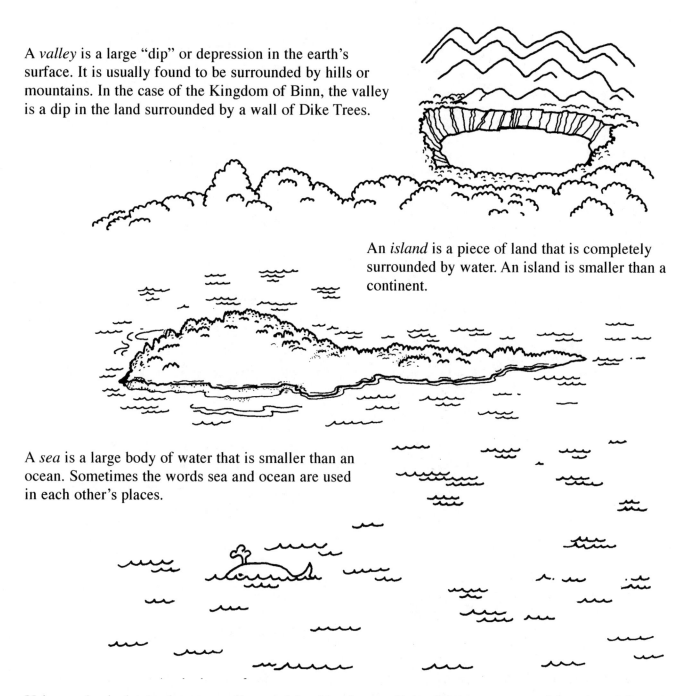

A *sea* is a large body of water that is smaller than an ocean. Sometimes the words sea and ocean are used in each other's places.

Using a physical map, locate a valley, an island, and a sea. Point them out to your classmates. After you have done this, draw your own picture that includes a valley, an island, and a sea. Label them with real or imagined names!

Geography Lesson

Here are some geographical terms that are not mentioned in The King's Stilts but are fun to learn.

A *mountain* is a mass of rock that has been thrust through the surface of the land because of the heat and pressure inside the earth. Mountains are high above the land that surrounds them.

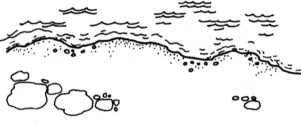

A *beach* is the land that is at the edge of an ocean, sea, or lake. It is usually sandy or rocky. A seashore is a type of beach.

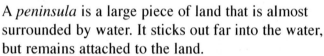

A *peninsula* is a large piece of land that is almost surrounded by water. It sticks out far into the water, but remains attached to the land.

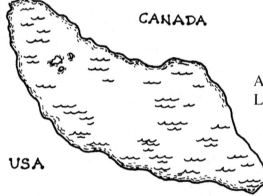

A *lake* is a body of water that is surrounded by land. Lakes are smaller than seas, but larger than ponds.

A *river* is a long, large stream of water that moves toward the lowest place. Rivers usually flow toward oceans, seas, lakes, or other streams.

Using a physical map, locate a mountain, a beach, a peninsula, a lake, and a river. Point them out to your classmates. After you have done this, draw your own picture that includes these things. Label them with real or imagined names!

Making Simple Stilts

King Birtram of the Kingdom of Binn loved to take his bright red stilts out of the tall stilt closet in the castle's front hallway and race about his kingdom with all the joy of a child. He had glorious fun atop his flashing red stilts!

Have you ever tried to walk on stilts? If you have, share your experience with your class.

Here are directions for making and using a simple pair of stilts.

Can Stilts

You will need:

- 2 same size cans (Coffee cans or large soup cans work well for this project.)

- a key-style can opener

- four yards of thin rope, cut into two yard lengths

Directions:

- Clean a pair of cans that are the same size.

- Use a key-type can opener to punch two holes in each can as shown in the diagram.

- Thread a length of thin rope through each can, gathering the ends together in a secure knot.

- Paint the stilts bright red. Allow the paint to dry.

- Step on the cans and walk! With patience and practice, perhaps you too can race your flashing red stilts about your "kingdom"!

The Lorax

by Dr. Seuss
(Available in U.S. and Canada from Random House, 1971)

Summary

In the midst of a dying and polluted town, a young boy searches for the reasons a creature named the Lorax was mysteriously lifted away so many years ago. He finds the answers from the old Once-ler, who tells a tale of greed and environmental death. The Lorax tried to stop the slow, steady destruction of the land around him, could not, and left. But, there is hope for the future, a future in which the young boy can play a major part. This is a poignant tale, pointing out the need to be ecologically aware.

Before Reading the Book

- Describe what you think a Lorax might be. You may use words and/or pictures.

- Brainstorm the ways trees can be used.

- Draw a picture of a brand new type of tree. Describe its special characteristics.

- Discuss ways people can harm and help Earth.

While Reading the Book

- Make a forest of Truffula Trees. (page 47)

- Have a "softness" display. Invite students to decide which of several materials is the softest. What do they think the tufts of the Truffula Tree would feel most like?

- Brainstorm Earth-friendly alternatives for Thneeds. (page 48)

- Draw the whole body of the Once-ler. (page 49)

- Compile a list of all the changes the Once-ler caused to happen in the world of the Lorax.

- Discuss the meaning of "UNLESS."

After Reading the Book

- Ask critical thinking questions, such as these:

  > "Why did the old Once-ler give the seed to the little boy?"

  > "Where did the Lorax go?"

  > "Do you think what the Once-ler family did was right?"

- What do you think might happen in the future if the story were to continue? Work in groups to create Part II.

- Compare the story with events that are occurring today in our world. (page 50)

- Read *The Great Kapok Tree* by Lynne Cherry. (HBJ, 1989)

- Compare the similarities and differences of the stories.

- What can you do to be ecologically aware? (page 51)

A Forest of Truffula Trees

Make a forest of Truffula Trees for your classroom. Use the pattern on this page to help you.

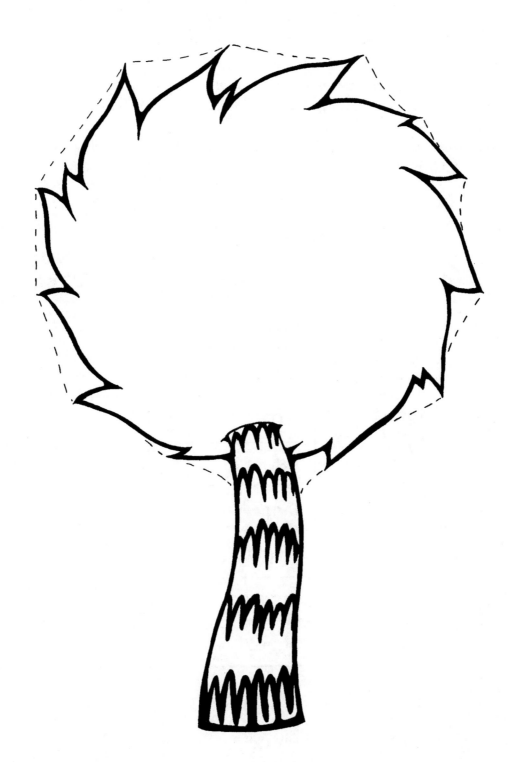

You can help create a forest of real trees, too. Contact your local parks department for places where kids are needed to help plant trees.

Thneed's

According to the Once-ler,

"A Thneed's a Fine-Something-That-All-People-Need!
It's a shirt. It's a sock. It's a glove. It's a hat.
But it has other uses. Yes, far beyond that.
You can use it for carpets. For pillows! For sheets!
Or curtains! Or covers for bicycle seats!"

Speak for the trees, as the Lorax does. Work by yourself, in groups, or as a class to brainstorm Earth-friendly alternatives for Thneeds.

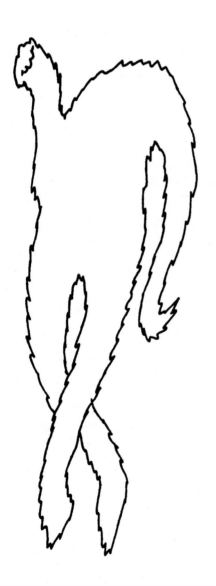

Thneed Use	Alternative for Thneed
shirt	
sock	
glove	
hat	
carpets	
pillows	
curtains	
sheets	
covers for bicycle seats	

So This is a Once-ler!

While you were reading *The Lorax*, did you ever wonder what the rest of the Once-ler looked like? Use this space to draw what you imagine the whole body of the Once-ler might look like.

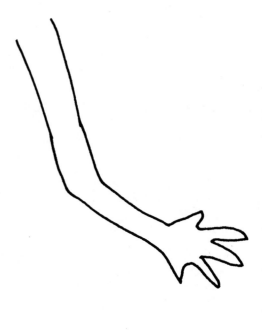
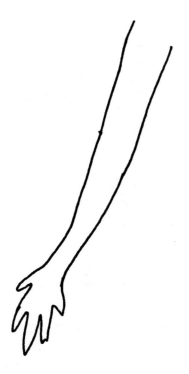

Fantasy and Reality

Some parts of *The Lorax* may remind you of things that you've seen or heard are going on in our world today. Draw lines to match the fantasy ideas of Dr. Seuss with the reality we know. Discuss the matching pairs in class.

What Can You Do?

"Now that you're here,
the word of the Lorax seems perfectly clear.
UNLESS someone like you
cares a whole awful lot,
nothing is going to get better.
It's not."
– Dr. Seuss

What can you do to help the environment? Brainstorm with your class for a list of ideas. Add them to the ones on this page. Then, working by yourself, with a partner, or as a class, choose an area, present an explanation of how doing this can help save Earth, plan a course of action, and do it!

- Recycle clear and colored glass.
- Do not buy overpackaged items.
- Make bird houses and feeders.
- Hang on to your helium balloons.
- Use scissors to snip six-pack rings.
- Water the yard efficiently.
- Use your own grocery bag.
- Wear a sweater inside when it's cold.
- Adopt an animal.
- Walk or ride a bike when possible.
- Decide what you want . . .
- Use rechargeable batteries.
- Buy toys that last.

- Recycle aluminum cans.
- Have a garage sale.
- Adopt a stream.
- Pick up litter.
- Plant a tree.
- Use cloth towels.
- Appreciate bugs.
- Create wildlife habitats.
- Turn off the lights.
- Save paper.
- Stop water leaks
- Share what you learn about ecology.

Many books have great ideas for ways kids can be involved in ecological issues. One great resource is *50 Simple Things Kids Can Do to Save the Earth* by John Javna. (Andrews and McMeel, 1990)

The 500 Hats of Bartholomew Cubbins

by Dr. Seuss
(Available in U.S. and Canada from Random House, 1938)

Summary

Although Bartholomew Cubbins removes his hat as the King passes by, another hat is still on his head. The King becomes angrier as each hat that Bartholomew removes reveals another underneath. Hats start to become fancier and fancier, until the 500th hat is so beautiful that the King wants to buy it for 500 pieces of gold.

Before Reading the Book

- Count to 500 by ones, by fives, by tens, by fifties, and by one hundreds.

- Build a line of 500 blocks or math cubes in your classroom.

- Ask students to collect 500 objects such as pennies, pasta, cereal, paper clips, or other small items. Organize and display collections so students can visualize the number 500.

- Bring in a collection of hats to the classroom. Include hats that would be worn by people in different occupations. Invite students to bring in hats, also. Discuss who would wear each hat. Classify hats into categories such as those worn by children or adults, hats worn in cold weather, hats worn for safety, and any of their own other ideas for categorizing. A follow-up activity can be found on page 53.

While Reading the Book

- Have students help Sir Alaric practice his counting. (page 54)

- Solve the hat word problems on page 55.

- Ask students to recall the ways the King tried to rid Bartholomew of his hats. Invite suggestions for other ways to rid the boy of his hats.

- Have students work together to make 500 hats. These hats can be displayed throughout the classroom to help students visualize the concept of 500 hats. (page 56)

After Reading the Book

- Create math problems to see which combinations make 500.

- Bartholomew's hats become more elaborate as he takes off hats number 450 and beyond. Make some hats to wear! (page 57) Decorations will make them spectacular!

- Do your students think the gold Bartholomew received will make any difference in his life or the life of his family?

- Predict what will happen the next time Bartholomew goes to town. Share stories as a class activity.

Who Wears This Hat?

Draw a line from each person to the hat that you think he or she would wear.

Help!

Help Sir Alaric count Bartholomew's hats. Write the correct numeral in each blank.

1. 3, 4, 5, _____

2. 9, 10, _____

3. 14, 15, _____

4. 21, 22, _____

5. 38, 39, _____

6. 50, 51, _____   11. 101, ____, 103, 104

7. 75, 76, _____   12. 216, 217, ____, 219

8. 80, 81, _____   13. 298, 299, ____, 301

9. 89, 90, _____   14. 349, ____, 351, 352

10. 98, 99, _____   15. 497, 498, 499, ____

In the space below, make up some of your own counting puzzles. Give what you have done to a classmate to solve.

Hat Problems!

Solve these hat problems. Remember to read each problem very carefully.

1. If Bartholomew took off 3 hats while the King watched, and the wind blew off 87 more, how many hats had come off the boy's head?

2. When Bartholomew got to the throne room, he took off 45 more hats. How many hats came off his head so far?

3. Sir Snipps knocked off one more of Bartholomew's hats, and the Grand Duke Wilfred shot off some more hats to bring the total to 154 hats. How many did the Grand Duke Wilfred shoot off?

4. The Yeoman of the Bowmen shot off 1 hat, Bartholomew left 178 more on the dungeon steps, and the executioner flipped off 13. If you add these hats together, how many do you have?

5. Bartholomew snatched off hats 347 to 450 on his way to be thrown from the highest turret. Then, the hats started to change. How many of the same hats did he snatch off?

6. After hat 450, all the ones that followed to 500 were different from each other. How many fancy hats were there in all?

500 Hats!

Work together to make 500 hats to be displayed throughout the classroom. This pattern can serve as the pattern for hats 1 to 450, then modified with materials for hats 451 to 500.

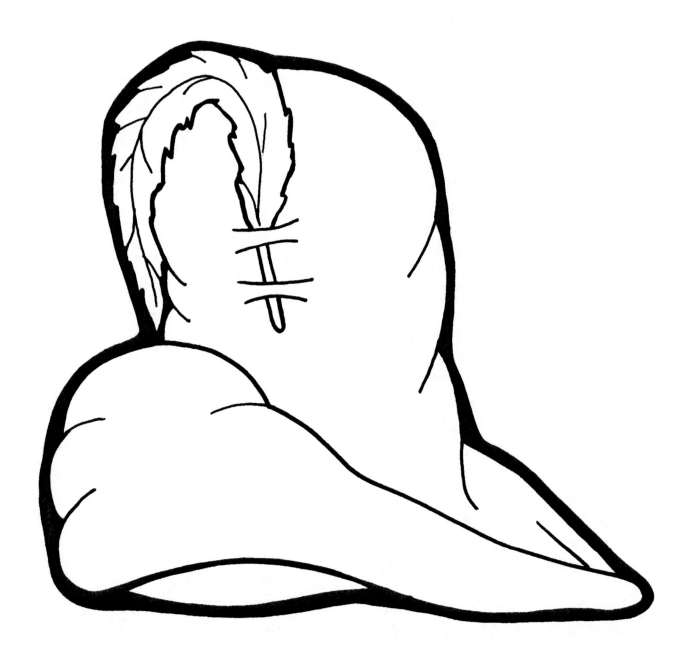

Paper Bag Hats

Quite impressive hats can be made of paper bags, classroom scraps, and imagination! Here are some ideas.

Materials Needed

- Brown paper bag (Many different sizes will work, but 8" x 14" [20 cm. x 35 cm] is the minimum size.)

- Tempera or poster paints

- Construction paper scraps

- A variety of lightweight items for trimming, such as feathers, buttons, ribbons, scraps of fabric, pipe cleaners, artificial flowers, sequins, lace, and beads. (You will probably want to begin this collection at least a week prior to making the hats.)

- White glue

Directions

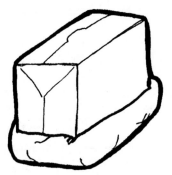

- Roll the sides of the bag down (going to the outside) a couple of inches at a time, until the desired size is reached. Try on the hat and adjust so the crown is the desired height.

- Paint the outside of the hat and let it dry. The dried paint will make the hat more sturdy.

- Add details to your hat. Use your imagination and the scrapbox to create trimmings for your hat. You might want to look at some of Bartholomew's ornate hats at the end of the book for inspiration. Hat bands can be made with ribbons, fabric scraps, or construction paper strips cut to size. Glue details in place and allow to dry.

- Curling feathers can be made by folding a strip of 3" x 9" (8 cm x 23 cm) paper in half lengthwise. Make parallel cuts slanting toward the fold. Then open and glue a pipe cleaner on the fold line. Trim and curl "feather" as you wish when it is dry. Stick it in your hat!

- Have a "Hat Parade" when you and your classmates are finished!

Scrambled Eggs Super!

by Dr. Seuss
(Available in U.S. and Canada from Random House, 1953)

Summary

Peter T. Hooper is tired of eating ordinary scrambled eggs. He searches far and wide to collect rare and unusual eggs so that he can concoct the most super scrambled egg dish ever. At the end of his quest, he scrambles his entire collection to create "Scrambled Eggs Super."

Before Reading the Book

- Brainstorm a list of words that have to do with eggs.

- Make a list of information the class already knows about eggs and a list of questions about eggs they would like to have answered.

- Check science texts and other references for basic information about birds.

- Gather books about birds from your school and public libraries to make a classroom collection. Have students team or work as individuals to choose a bird to research and share what they have learned with the class. Drawings of birds and eggs should be included in the presentation.

- Discuss the kinds of foods children eat for breakfast. Ask students to describe how they or their parents make scrambled eggs. Compare different techniques and recipes. Explain to the class that they will be reading a story about a boy who concocted a very unusual batch of scrambled eggs.

While Reading the Book

- Have students help Peter T. Hooper find a most amazing egg by creating mazes for each other to complete.

- Encourage students to wash, save, and bring eggshells from home for an eggshell mosaic art activity. (page 59)

After Reading the Book

- Visit museums or science centers that have collections of birds and eggs.

- Go for a walk to collect bird nest materials to make the nest described on page 61.

- Enjoy the creative movement activity on page 62.

- Make "Scrambled Eggs Super." (recipe on page 63)

- Read *Green Eggs and Ham* by Dr. Seuss.

- Read *Chickens Aren't the Only Ones* by Ruth Heller (Grosset & Dunlap, 1981). Discuss other animals that lay eggs. (page 60)

Eggshell Art

These eggshell mosaics make colorful displays in the Spring!

Directions:

1. Ask children to wash and save eggshells from home in an egg carton.

2. When each child has collected one dozen eggshells, have children bring their containers and shells to school.

3. Direct children to paint the shells with watercolors.

4. they have dried, break the shells into pieces and sort by color into empty egg carton compartments.

5. Choose an egg shape from this page or one of your own that is the best size for the ability level of your students.

6. Ask students to draw designs on the egg shapes to be filled mosaic-style with the bits of colored eggshells.

7. Apply glue to small areas and gently press the colored egg-shell into the glue.

8. Allow the eggshell designs time to dry completely.

9. Display the eggshell art in individual baskets, a group egg-carton, or on a nature-filled bulletin board.

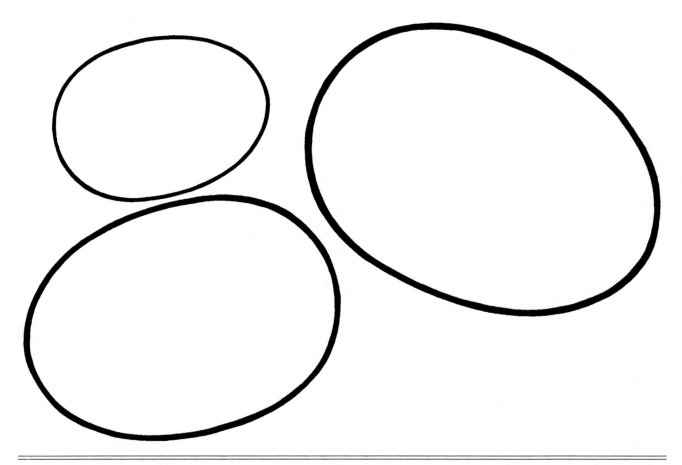

Birds Aren't the Only Ones!

Whose eggs are these? Draw a line from the animals to their eggs. Color the pictures.

Make a Bird's Nest!

Ask students to bring their lunch to school in a brown paper bag. After lunch, go for a short walk, and use the empty lunch bag to collect items that a bird might use to build its nest. (You might want to put out some yarn ahead of time.) Children can collect twigs, grass, yarn, string, leaves, or anything else they might find on the ground. Remind them to harm no living thing during the collection process.

Once you return to the classroom, show students how to roll the top of the paper bag down to shape a bird's nest. Ask them to arrange the materials they have collected inside the bag nest.

Shape eggs out of modeling clay or cut construction paper ovals and paint or color these eggs for your nest.

Make a bird for your nest from construction paper scraps or use this bird pattern. Color your bird, cut it out, and place it in your nest!

Spread Your Wings!

For this creative movement activity, select music that starts out slowly, and gradually becomes faster paced. Vivaldi's "Four Seasons" is one composition that has been used successfully for this activity.

Have children begin this activity on the floor, with their bodies tucked into an "egg" position. Knees should be tucked in, foreheads on the floor, and "wings" (arms) at their sides.

Start the music and talk about how a baby bird might feel. Children should dramatize a bird's actions as you talk.

Here is a sample dialogue.

"The baby birds inside the eggs try to move but can't. They stretch and push against the shell. They peck at the shells, trying to break through."

"Crack! Crack! Crack! Crack!"

"Tiny birds peek out and look around, slowly emerging from their shells."

"The birds gradually make their way out and peep for their mother to feed them. They try to flap their wings."

"Mother bird brings her babies food. They open their beaks wide."

"The baby birds grow and grow. They spread their wings and try to fly. They are not babies any longer."

"The birds fly around the room."

"Now, the birds are tired and come back to the nest to rest. They settle down, tucking their heads under their wings and go to sleep."

Time to Cook!

How do you like your scrambled eggs? Are you hungry for some right now? It's time to cook! Before you begin, what do you think are some of the ingredients and equipment that are necessary for making scrambled eggs?

_____   _____

_____   _____

_____   _____

What are some ingredients you like to add to your scrambled eggs?

_____

_____

_____

Recipe for your Scrambled Eggs Super!

This recipe will give 30 students a taste of scrambled eggs.

You will need:

- 2 dozen large eggs
- 1½ cups (375 mL) milk
- margarine, butter, or cooking oil to lightly cover pan bottom
- Pita bread, crackers, or bread
- various egg toppings, such as cheese, chives, bacon bits

- a large mixing bowl
- a whisk
- a pan
- a bag or plate for shells
- a serving spoon

Directions:

- Ask an adult to supervise your cooking.
- Wash your hands thoroughly.
- Break eggs into a large mixing bowl. Save the eggshells for the egg mosaic art project described on page 59.
- Add milk and stir with a whisk or a fork.
- Melt margarine or butter, or pour oil to lightly cover the bottom of the pan.
- Add egg mixture to pan and cook on low-medium heat until the eggs are done.

Serve each child a spoonful or two of eggs on a cracker or bread piece. Offer a "topping" bar to make the scrambled eggs "super."

Bartholomew and the Oobleck

by Dr. Seuss
(Available in U.S. and Canada from Random House, 1949)

Summary

The King who ruled the Kingdom of Didd was bored with ordinary sunshine, rain, fog, and snow. To make his weather-watching more interesting, he commanded his Royal Magicians to bring something new from the sky. His command greatly worried Bartholomew, the page boy. The boy's worries were confirmed when the Royal Magicians' magic spell produced sticky, green Oobleck, first in tiny green drops, but then in great globs which stuck to everything, covering the entire kingdom. The young page boy convinced the King to say "I'm sorry," and these words halted and melted the 'Oobleck'.

Before Reading the Book

- Discuss weather and the ways it affects our daily lives. Make a class or individual weather graph each week. (page 65) Keep track of local weather for one month and ask students to analyze the data they collected. Ask questions such as "Did we have more sunny days than cloudy days in March?"

- Brainstorm as many different words associated with weather as possible. Write them on a large sheet of butcher paper taped to the chalkboard. Categorize by circling related words with different colors of markers.

- Introduce reading a weather thermometer. Measure temperature in the shade and in the sun. Keep a record of the different temperatures. Discuss temperature as it relates to weather. (page 66)

- Ask children to talk about and draw a picture of their favorite kind of weather. (page 67)

While Reading the Book

- Instruct students to divide a large sheet of drawing paper into four sections and draw the same simple landscape in each section. Label each area sunshine, rain, fog, or snow. (Page 68 has a prepared picture.) Students will then color the pictures to show the differences in the weather.

- Ask critical thinking questions as you read the story, such as "Why do you think the King was angry at the sky?" "Did the Royal Magicians know what Oobleck was before they made it?" "How does Bartholomew feel about the King's command?"

- Have students pantomime being subjects in the Kingdom of Didd when the tiny drops of Oobleck began to fall and show what happened as the drops got larger and larger. Pantomime what happened when the Oobleck melted away.

After Reading the Book

- Make Oobleck and have students try to discover its different properties. (page 69)

- Ask students to imagine what it would be like if Oobleck started to fall from the sky in their neighborhood, and write a story about what they imagine.

- When the King said he was sorry, the sun began to shine, the Oobleck stopped falling and the Oobleck that was stuck on everything in the kingdom melted away. Ask your students to think of a time when they said, "I'm sorry," and to share what happened because of these words.

Weather Graph

Weather Graph

for

_____

Observe the weather each day and color in a box to make your weather graph.

Weather	Recording Boxes				
 sunny					
 cloudy					
 rainy					
 snowy					
foggy					

Temperatures Around Me

Check the temperature of several different places or the same place at different times. Color in the thermometers to show the temperatures.

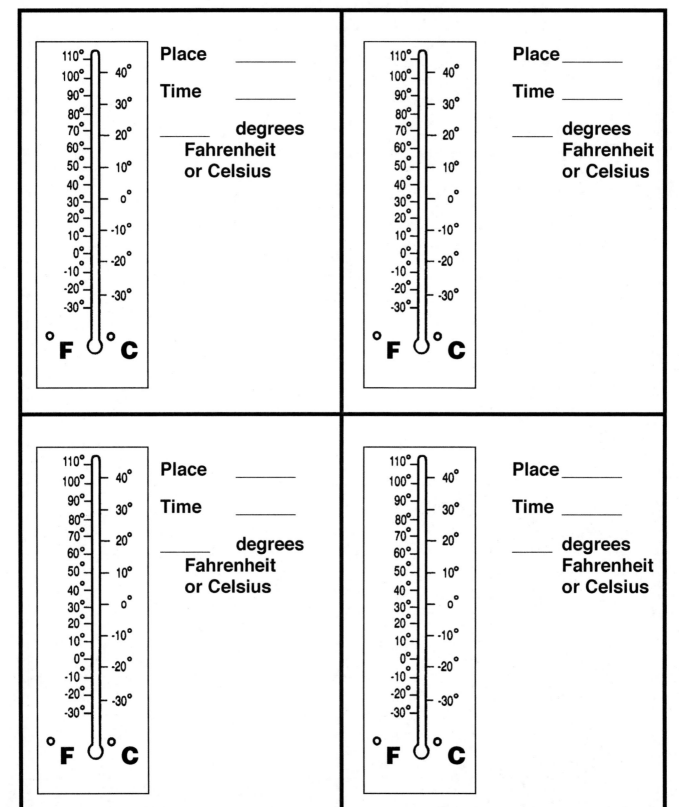

My Favorite Weather

Draw a picture of your favorite kind of day. Color in the thermometer to show what temperature you enjoy on your favorite day.

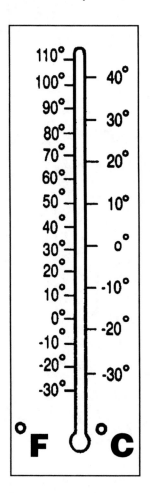

My favorite kind of day is a(n) _____ day.

Picture the Weather!

Color each picture to show the weather differences.

Sunny	**Rainy**
Foggy	**Snowy**

Oobleck!

This recipe will make enough "Oobleck" for a class of 30.

You will need:

a large mixing bowl

mixing spoon

green food coloring

10 cups (2½ L) of cornstarch

6 cups (1½ L) of room temperature water

Directions:

Put water in the large bowl and add food coloring drop by drop until the water is an "Oobleck" green. Mix in cornstarch a cup at a time. Mix thoroughly. Have reserve box of cornstarch to use for thickening the mixture if it is too fluid to handle.

Individual batches can be made in paper cups and stirred with plastic spoons or popsicle sticks. Use about ½ cup (125 mL) of cornstarch to nearly ¼ cup (50 mL) of water. Thicken with more cornstarch if necessary.

Now what can we do?

- Try to make it into a ball. Does it bounce?
- Try to pull it apart, slowly and quickly.
- Hold it in your hand and see what happens.
- Does it stick to your desk?
- Try some more Oobleck experiments!

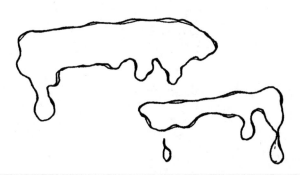

Hop on Pop

by Dr. Seuss
(Available in U.S. and Canada from Random House, 1963)

Summary

Hop on Pop *is not one story, but a collection of little stories based around a rhyming idea. With these simple rhymes and charming illustrations, Dr. Seuss gives beginning readers a chance to be successful readers.*

Before Reading the Book

- Discuss what makes a rhyme. (page 71)

- Play rhyming games. For example, student #1 thinks of a word and student #2 thinks of a rhyme to go with it. Student #3 tries to think of a different rhyme to go with the pattern. The game continues until all possibilities are exhausted. Then, a student chooses a new word for the game. Keep track of the number of rhymes found for each word.

- Make rhyme lists. Add to these lists as your students think of new words. If you post the lists, they can help students in their reading and writing fluency. (pages 72 and 73)

- Ask students for their predictions about the contents of the book after they have seen the cover and read the title.

While Reading the Book

- Throughout your reading, ask students to make a list of words they can read by themselves. When you finish the book, students can make up their own stories using the word lists they have created.

- As you read all, a few, or one of the rhyming stories, cover the part of the story that is in smaller print. See if your students can guess what Dr. Seuss might have written using the rhyming words printed in capitals.

- Discuss the content of each story.

After Reading the Book

- After reading each story, ask students what would be on the next page if the story were to continue. Remind them that they have to continue the rhyme pattern!

- Practice matching rhymes. (pages 74 and 75)

- Make simple rhyming stories such as those found in *Hop on Pop*. Ask students to create these stories as individuals, in small groups, or as a class. After each story is completed, it may be student illustrated and bound in a class book of rhyming stories!

What Makes a Rhyme?

Rhyme happens when words are repeated that sound alike. Snake and cake, book and cook, rattle and battle, will and spill, and flower and power are all examples of words that rhyme.

Unscramble these words into lists that rhyme.

spent	match	pick	hand	shook
hatch	stick	tent	brick	band
book	stand	batch	hook	rent

LIST 1	LIST 2	LIST 3	LIST 4	LIST 5
sent	*scratch*	*trick*	*land*	*took*
_____	_____	_____	_____	_____
_____	_____	_____	_____	_____
_____	_____	_____	_____	_____

Fill in these shapes with rhyming words.

Rhyme Headings

Color and cut out these headings to use on your own paper or poster board as you brainstorm class rhyme lists. Encourage your students to think of multiple syllable rhymes as well, such as round, surround, underground, or take, mistake, rattlesnake!

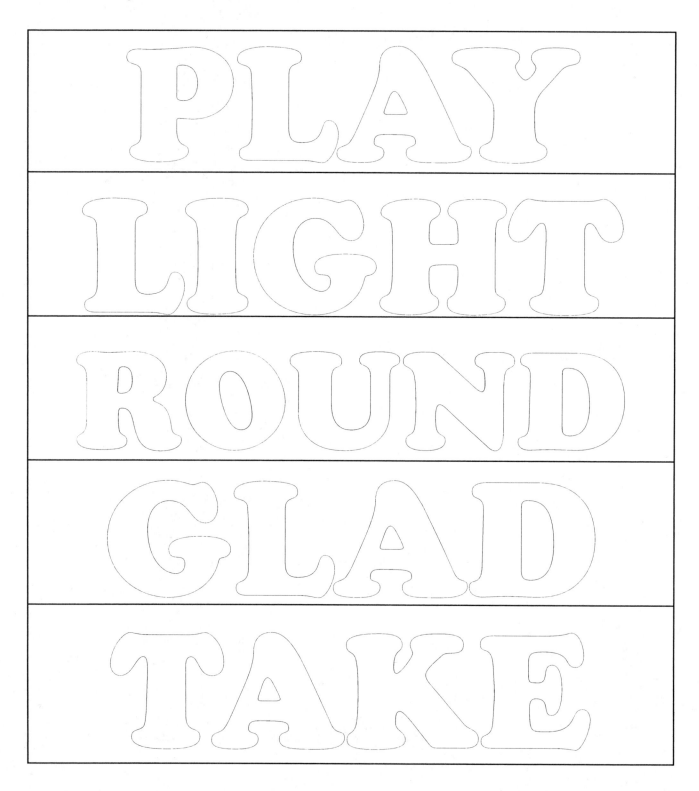

Rhyme Headings

Color and cut out these headings to use on your own paper or poster board as you brainstorm class rhyme lists. Encourage your students to think of multiple syllable rhymes as well, such as small, rainfall, basketball or tree, teepee, guarantee!

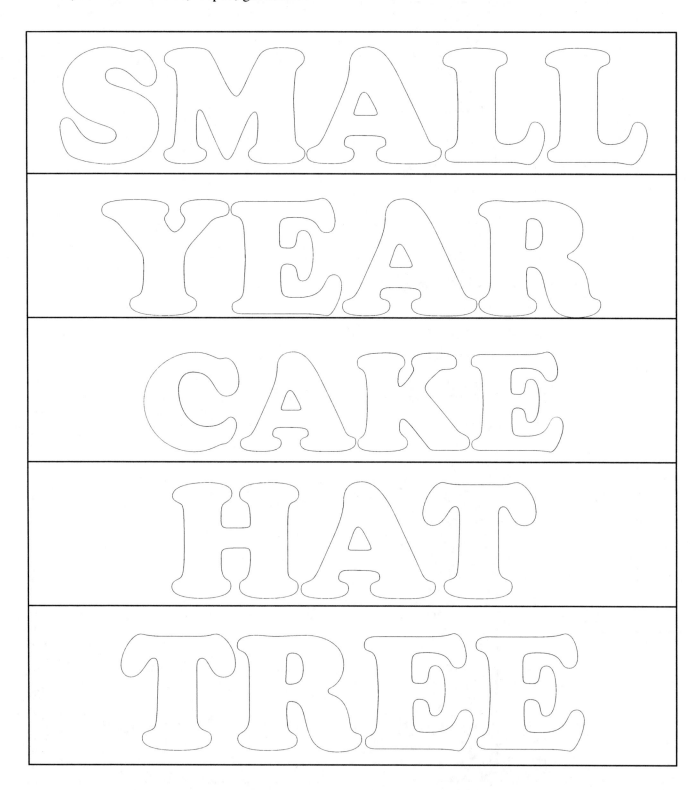

Match the Rhymes!

Cut these words apart and match them with their rhymes on page 75.

rake	small	trick	hop
bunny	spell	coaster	pen
plant	brought	three	will
wrong	think	swing	mouse
night	play	seat	book
sad	splat	flower	cup
chair	sand	toy	nail

Match the Rhymes!

Cut these words apart and match them with their rhymes on page 74.

cake	tall	brick	shop
funny	smell	toaster	hen
ant	thought	knee	hill
strong	pink	bring	house
right	stay	treat	cook
glad	flat	power	pup
stair	band	joy	snail

If I Ran the Zoo

by Dr. Seuss
(Available in U.S. and Canada from Random House, 1950)

Summary

When Gerald McGrew visits the zoo, he begins to imagine what it would be like if he ran the zoo. He describes all the amazing and wonderful animals that he would capture.

Before Reading the Book

- Ask students if they have ever been to the zoo. Brainstorm a list of as many different zoo animals as they can think of. Write the names on cards or pocket chart strips and classify animals by class, by continent, by color, by first letter of their names, etc. Ask your students for more ideas for ways they can sort the cards.

- Share ideas of unusual zoo animals. Encourage students to discuss what makes these choices unusual.

- Gather a classroom collection of zoo animal books.

While Reading the Book

- Call attention to the details that make each of the animals unique. Look for similarities and differences.

- Start with drawings of zoo animals and add details that would transform them into animals that Gerald McGrew would consider for his zoo. (page 77)

- Make a flip book that allows children to vary three sections of animals to make many different and unusual combinations. (pages 78 and 79)

- Ask students to write a letter to Gerald McGrew telling him about an amazing animal that he might want for his zoo and to draw a picture of the animal to enclose with their letters. (page 80)

- Make a classroom "McGrew's Zoo" filled with modeling clay animals the students have created. Have available a variety of materials that student sculptors can use to add details to their animals, such as feathers, yarn, beads, pasta, etc.

- Have students use an atlas or map to find place names that can be matched with imaginative animal names, as Dr. Seuss does.

After Reading the Book

- Provide large paper for students to create imaginary zoo animals, using black crayon to outline the animal first. Then, they can fill in the inside areas with watercolor, tissue paper collage, or bright tempera paints. Ask students to describe the animals they have created, recording the details on an information sheet that can be displayed and/ or shared together with the animal picture in the class. Include the animal's name, habitat, description, habits, and other specific details in the information sheet.

- Invite children to design stand-up construction paper animals using a basic body shape that can be free cut as shown in the example on page 81. They can add details made by paper sculpture techniques, such as fringing, scoring, pleating, curling, and hole-punching.

- Ask your students if they think a zoo of unusual animals would be an exciting place to visit and if such a zoo would be possible. Encourage discussion.

- Plan a trip to the zoo.

How About This?

Transform this animal into one you think Gerald McGrew would want for his zoo!

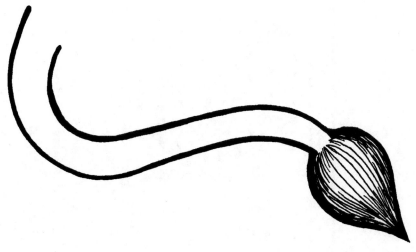

Zany Animal Flip Book

Here are some animals Gerald McGrew might love for his zoo. Make a flip book to create even more combinations for his collection!

Color the animals on this page. Cut out each rectangle. Attach all "pages" together with brads at the marked holes. Then, snip each page into thirds by cutting on the broken lines.

Zany Animal Flip Book

Here are some animals Gerald McGrew might love for his zoo. In the last boxes, design some of your own animals for the flip book!

A Letter to McGrew

Gerald McGrew wants unique and amazing animals for his zoo. Write a letter to him telling about an animal that you think he would like to have in his zoo. Also include a drawing of your animal in the letter. Your letter could look something like this:

Date

Dear Gerald McGrew,

In this paragraph, tell Gerald about the animal you would like him to have in his zoo. Describe the animal in detail, including its name, habitat, habits, and unique characteristics.

In this paragraph, try to convince Gerald why this animal would be a good addition to his zoo.

In this paragraph, tell him how he can get this animal if he is interested.

You might end your letter something like this:

I hope you will have a(n) _____
_ in your zoo next time I visit. I know other children will enjoy this animal as much as I do.

Sincerely,

Your Name

Remember to use capital letters for names and the beginnings of sentences. Exchange letters with a friend for proofreading.

Stand-Up Animals

Materials:

One 4" x 5½" (10 cm x 14 cm) piece of construction paper for body; one 2" x 3" (5 cm x 8 cm) piece of construction paper for head; scraps of construction paper - all colors; scraps of yarn and string - many colors; scissors; crayons or markers; white glue or paste

Procedure:

1. Body - Fold the 4" x 5½" construction paper in half, widthwise. Cut out a half oval from the center of the open edges as illustrated.

2. Head - Fold the 2" x 3" paper in half either lengthwise or widthwise. Cut as illustrated.

   Add details with crayons, markers, paper scraps, yarn, string, etc, to head and body.

3. Glue head to body.

Variations:

After cutting the half-oval in Step 1 above, open the paper and lay flat. Cut 1/2" (1.25 cm) slit on each side of the center fold as shown. Fold up along each side to make the legs. Now it can stand up.

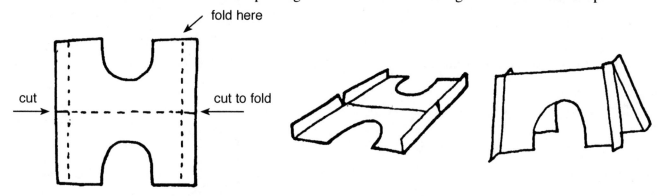

Variations:

For birds, reptiles, insects, fish, etc., vary the technique to match the body shape of the animal. For example, a crocodile might begin with a 5" x 8" (13 cm x 20 cm) piece of construction paper folded in half lengthwise.

Horton Hears a Who!

by Dr. Seuss
(Available in U.S. and Canada from Random House, 1954)

Summary

Horton's happy splashing in a jungle pool stopped when he heard a faint cry for help. Upon further investigation, he was amazed to discover a community of tiny creatures called Whos living on a dust speck hurtling to their doom. Horton rescued them, gently placing their tiny dust speck on a clover blossom. He resolved to protect them, for "a person's a person, no matter how small." However, his jungle friends could not hear the Whos, and ridiculed Horton, whisking the clover from his protection. But, the elephant's dedication to equality persisted, and how the Whos were heard and saved, points out the significance of every living being.

Before Reading the Book

- Discuss the concept of equality. *Horton Hears a Who!* would be an excellent book to use before, during, or after any unit that focuses on equality.

- Order pictures in the order of small, smaller, and smallest. (page 83)

- Ask students for their ideas of what a Who could be before they read the book. Invite them to draw their ideas.

While Reading the Book

- After reading the first three pages, close the book. Imagine the type of creatures that could exist on a speck of dust. Draw their world.

- Put a speck of dust on a microscope slide and examine it.

- Collect several clover blossoms. Investigate them with your senses.

- Populate the Whoville model with Whos. (page 84)

- Complete the "A person's a person, no matter how small" graphic on page 85.

After Reading the Book

- Discuss the concept of democracy.

- Predict the future of the Whos under their new "jungle protection plan."

- Study jungle animals and environments.

- Create an Opinion Board where all ideas are valued. (pages 86 and 87)

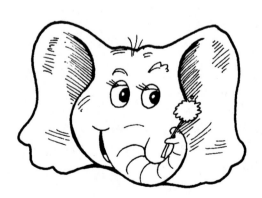

Small, Smaller, Smallest

Color the groupings of animals and things on this page. Cut them out and arrange them in the order of small, smaller, smallest.

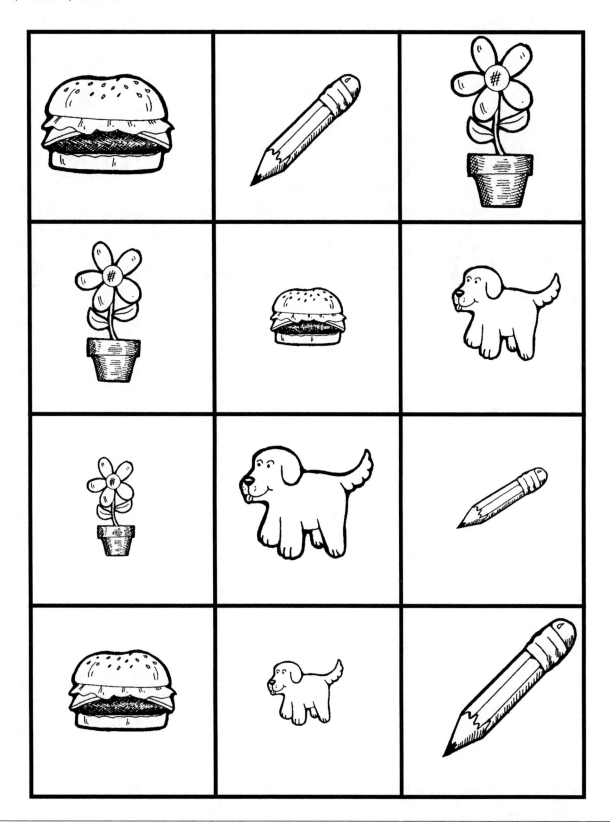

What's in Whoville?

Without Horton, the Whos in Whoville would have died. It might have looked as empty as the Whoville on this page. Fill up Whoville by drawing Whos doing Who things!

Color, cut out, and display this graphic to help you remember the ideas in *Horton Hears a Who!*

"A Person's a Person, No Matter How Small"

Everyone's Opinion Is Important!

Horton knows and helps teach others that all people, no matter how small, are important and have the right to be here. It doesn't matter if we are old or young, rich or poor, dark-skinned or light skinned, or tall or small. We all are IMPORTANT and so are our OPINIONS!

Collect answers to the questions on the cards below and on page 87. Be sure to include answers from many different types of people.

When you have your survey results back, post the cards on a large bulletin board display with the title:

"A Person's a Person, No Matter How Small."

Person: _____ **Questions:** What scares you? **Answer:**	**Person:** _____ **Questions:** If you could live anywhere, where would you live? **Answer:**
Person: _____ **Questions:** What would you do with a hundred dollars? **Answer:**	**Person:** _____ **Questions:** What would you do if you could do anything you wanted to do? **Answer:**

Person: _____

Questions: What makes you
happiest?

Answer:

Person: _____

Questions: What do you enjoy
doing outdoors?

Answer:

Person: _____

Questions: What makes you
feel sad?

Answer:

Person: _____

Questions: What is the sport you
enjoy playing more than
any other?

Answer:

Person: _____

Questions: What about your best
friend do you like
the most?

Answer:

Person: _____

Questions: Who is your favorite
story character?

Answer:

The Butter Battle Book

by Dr. Seuss
(Available in U.S. and Canada from Random House, 1984)

Summary

The Yooks eat their bread butter side up. The Zooks eat their bread butter side down. This difference between them is enough to create a war. In The Butter Battle Book, *Dr. Seuss gives his readers a stark look at the major conflicts minor differences can cause.*

Before Reading the Book

- Ask students to brainstorm a list of things that cause people to fight. For an added challenge, ask them to arrange them in an order of most common to least common reasons. (page 89)

- Read the title of the book. Do not show the cover. Ask students to guess what the book will be about.

- Bring bread and butter to school. Ask for three or four volunteers to butter a slice of bread with their own style of buttering. Discuss differences and similarities.

While Reading the Book

- See if students understand who started the battle.

- Divide the class into ten groups. Each group designs and draws one of the weapons used in *The Butter Battle Book.* (Snick-Berry Switch; Slingshot; Triple-Sling Jigger; Jigger-Rock Snatchem; Kick-a-Poo Kid; Eight-Nozzled, Elephant-Toted Boom-Blitz; Yook Utterly Sputter; Zook Utterly Sputter; Yook Bitsy Big-Boy Boomeroo; Zook Bitsy Big-Boy Boomeroo) After the pictures are drawn, students can order the weapons in the sequence they were used in the story.

- Discuss the escalation of wars.

- Ask students to explain the ending.

After Reading the Book

- Predict what would come next if the story continued.

- As a class, think of ways the butter battle could have been avoided. Ask students to choose the two ways they believe are the best and print each way on squares of yellow construction paper approximately 2" x 2" (5 cm x 5 cm). Show the bread pattern on page 90, and ask your students to make a piece of bread out of cardboard, tag, or other heavy material. Students can "butter" both sides of their "bread" with two ways to avoid battle. Bread slices can be suspended from the ceiling, a wire, or a rod so that both reasons and both buttered sides of the bread, can be easily seen.

- Discuss ways to handle conflict. (page 91)

Why Fight?

Write your ideas about why people fight.

Choose four of the ideas from your list and put them in the order of most common to least common reasons to fight.

1. _____

2. _____

3. _____

4. _____

A Slice of Bread

Use with activity described on page 88.

Ways to Resolve Conflict

There are ways the Yooks and the Zooks could have handled their conflict peacefully. If they had known some of these ways, perhaps there never would have been a better butter battle.

1. SAY YOU ARE SORRY. Sometimes these words are the only thing the other person needs. Sometimes an explanation of why you are sorry will help, too.

2. COUNT TO 10 (or 15 or 20!) This gives you time to cool down a bit and a chance to think before you act. Think about the different choices you have in the situation. Think about the consequences of the different actions you could take. Decide which choice of action is the best for you.

3. TAKE TURNS TELLING EACH SIDE OF THE PROBLEM. Let the other person go first. Let the person finish all he or she has to say. Then you take your turn. You might start out by saying something like, "Why are you mad?"

4. HAVE ANOTHER PERSON YOU BOTH RESPECT HELP YOU SETTLE IT. Another person can often help you both see the other person's point of view.

5. MAKE A JOKE ABOUT THE SITUATION, so the other person will not take the conflict so seriously. Laughter eases many tensions.

6. WALK AWAY! This is sometimes hard to do, especially if other people are watching to see what you will do.

7. STAY OUT OF TROUBLE. Remember, the best way to keep a conflict from happening is to avoid it in the first place. Be aware of how your actions might look to others. Be careful not to hurt people's feelings or embarrass them.

Oh, the Places You'll Go!

by Dr. Seuss
(Available in U.S. and Canada from Random House, 1990)

Summary

In this guide to a youths journey through life, Dr. Seuss includes advice and encouragement in a positive, humorous style.

Before Reading the Book

- On a large world map, locate and place a marker at the birthplace of each child in the class. Trace any long trip that children have taken.

- Discuss feelings at the beginning of a new school year, the start of a vacation or trip, when moving to a different neighborhood or a new house, and making new friends. Ask children to tell or write about a time in their lives when they were at the beginning of something new or at a time of change.

- Ask children to construct a timeline of their lives in terms of milestones and important events.

While Reading the Book

- Guide the reading of this book with a suggestion that the readers imagine themselves in the child's place. Ask thought-provoking questions, such as "How would you feel if this child was you?" Read to find out the choices he will make.

- Discuss the waiting place. Ask children to make a list of at least ten things that they wait for. Compare lists and find common items.

- Ask students to do a quick write on a place they have been or would like to go.

After Reading the Book

- Have children research careers they are interested in and report their findings to the class.

- Invite guests of different occupations to visit your class to share the paths their lives have taken, what they had to do to prepare for their careers, and important decisions they have made.

- Students in cooperative groups could develop board games based on *Oh, The Places You'll Go!* or adapt the game on pages 93 to 97, adding their own details and game cards if they wish. Patterns may be enlarged and pages colored and laminated for durability.

- Make a wishing tree. Use a large branch for a class tree or make individual trees with twigs, paper cups, and modeling clay. Have students write personal goals and hopes for the future on slips of colored paper and fasten them to the tree. Encourage children to talk about their goals and plans for the future.

Oh, the Places You'll Go! Game

Game Instructions

1. Make and laminate the game board on pages 94 and 95 or create a game board of your own.

2. Use a button or coin for a game piece. You may play with two to four players.

3. Roll a die to determine who will go first. The person with the highest number is first, and then the order shifts clock-wise to the right.

4. Each roll of the die shows players how many spaces to move.

5. When you pass through a crossroads, you may move in any direction.

6. When you land on a crossroads square, take a crossroads card (pages 96 and 97) and follow the instructions on the card.

7. Two players game pieces may occupy the same square.

8. Decide at the beginning of the game how long you will play. Have one player keep time. Fifteen minutes is a good amount of time for a start.

9. Players move their game pieces until time is up. When time is called, the square you have landed on is your career choice.

10. You must tell the other players why the career you have "won" is "perfect" for you! You may have to make up some reasons!

Game Board

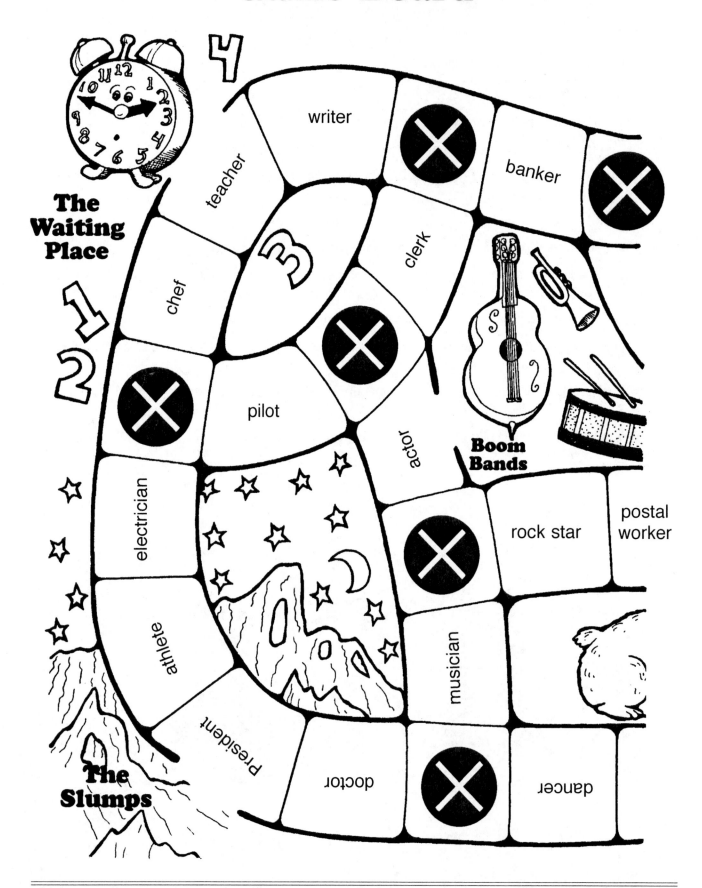

Game Board

See directions on page 93.

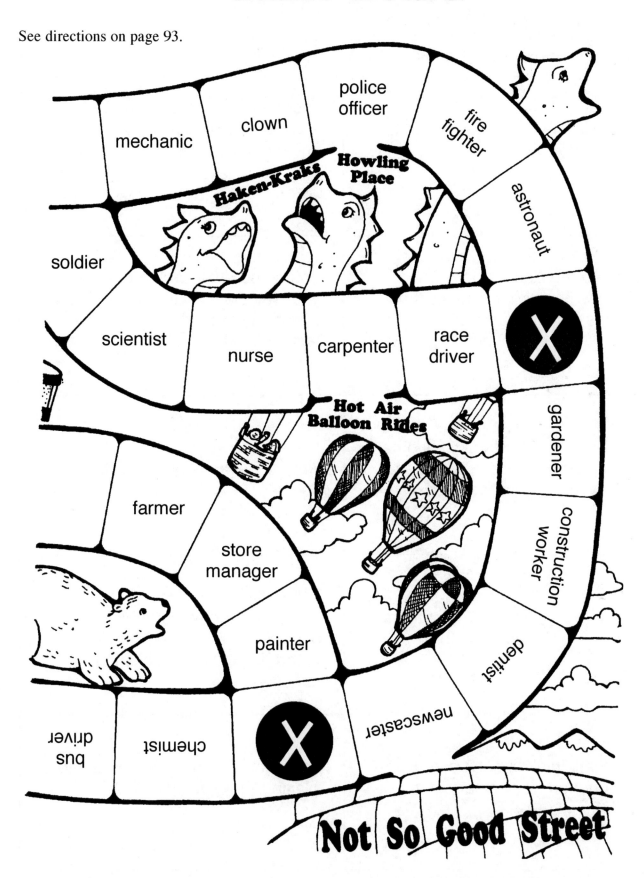

mechanic

clown

police officer

fire fighter

astronaut

soldier

Haken-Kraks

Howling Place

scientist

nurse

carpenter

race driver

X

gardener

Hot Air Balloon Rides

construction worker

farmer

store manager

painter

dentist

newscaster

X

bus driver

chemist

Not So Good Street

Crossroads Cards

Cut these cards apart on the dark lines and place them in a stack on the game board. Draw one card when a player lands on a crossroads square.

You step with care. Move ahead one square.	Today is your day! Tell players what made today so special. Move to a square with any career you would love.
Listen to the Boom Boom Bands and move toward the music three squares. Tell others what kind of music you are hearing.	You faced a big problem. Good for you! Tell players a problem you might have faced. Take an extra turn.
You're on the right track. Tell others what kind of job you would like to have. Move ahead five squares.	It is a beautiful day. Go to the Hot Air Balloons and soar to any square.
You have a good idea. Tell others what it is. Take an extra turn.	You make a new friend. Explain one thing that is important in a friend. Move two spaces in any direction.
You didn't think about it carefully. Wait one turn to think about it again.	You get stuck in traffic. Go to the Waiting Place for one turn.

Crossroads Cards *(Cont.)*

You're out of money. Go to the Slumps for two turns. Tell others three ways you could earn more money.	You were rude to a friend. Say something nice to every game player.
You change your mind. Go back the way you came four spaces.	Choose a career that is touching the square you are on. Tell everyone at the gameboard which one is your favorite and why.
You tripped on a shoelace you forgot to tie. Re-tie everyone's shoes at your gameboard and lose one turn.	You've done a fantastic job! Tell others one thing you do well. Take an extra turn.
You did your homework and no one else did. Everyone except you must go to The Slumps and lose one turn.	You make a silly mistake. Tell others what it was and go to the Hakken-Kraks' Howling Place to wait a turn.
You made a wrong turn and ended up on Not So Good Street. Wait patiently until another player lands on a crossroads square.	Go to the Boom Bands and listen to music. While you are listening, show players how well you dance!

Mulberry Street

For this culminating activity, students will have the opportunity to change their classroom into Mulberry Street! Here are a few of the many activities that can make the transformation possible!

* As a class, reread the book and brainstorm ways to make the classroom alive in Seuss-ish Mulberry Street style. Some ideas are provided on page 99.

* Color and cut a bulletin board heading of letters making the book's title. (pages 100 and 101)

* Construct a Mulberry Street street sign out of wrapping paper rolls, lightweight wood or cardboard, crepe paper, and other suitable materials.

* Make a large wagon from the model on page 102. It is quite effective if the model is three-dimensional, utilizing any available building materials, cardboard, paper-maché, and paper sculpturing techniques. Use the wagon as a centerpiece of all that will come imaginatively alive around it.

* Encourage the students to work as individuals or in small groups to fill their Mulberry Street with unique vehicles pulled by whatever they imagine might pull them. Their vehicles could be driven by their own characters who look like they might have come from a Dr. Seuss book. Encourage your students to give their characters and vehicles Seuss-like names and label them for others to enjoy.

* Make some mulberry trees by twisting brown paper bags for trunks and branches, adding elongated, heart-shaped leaves cut for green paper. (page 103)

* Make an old-fashioned mailbox out of a cardboard box with a slit for mail delivery. Paint it in vivid Seuss colors. In the mailbox, each child can post a letter of recommendation to a friend about one of his or her favorite Dr. Seuss books. Daily, the teacher or students can read a few book evaluation letters to the class.

* Invite students to cover the wall with rhymes about the sights they see on Mulberry Street.

* Send out invitations for others at the school to visit your Mulberry Street. (page 104)

Mulberry Street (cont.)

Here is just a sample of what the Culminating Activity could look like.

Letters for Bulletin Board
Heading

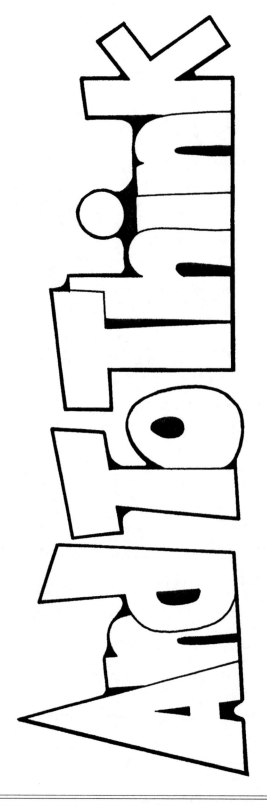

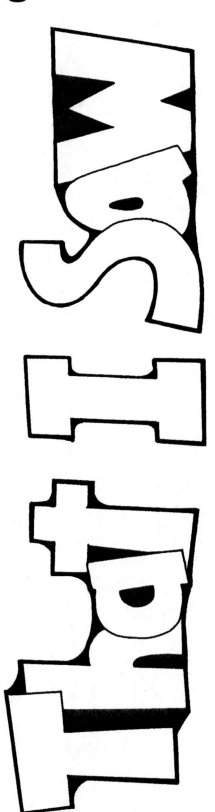

Letters for Bulletin Board
Heading *(cont.)*

The Wagon

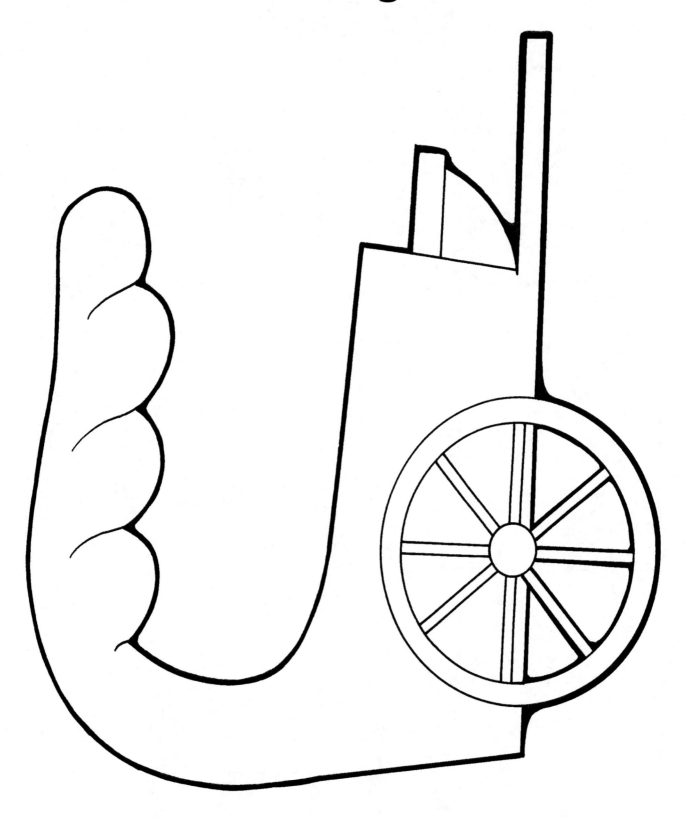

Mulberry Leaves

Use these mulberry leaves to place on your paper bag tree.

Invitation

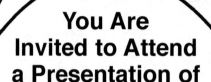

**You Are
Invited to Attend
a Presentation of**

And To Think That I Saw It On Mulberry Street

by

_____

on this date and time

_____

at this place

_____

We will read, rhyme, act, draw,
dance, and imagine our way
down Mulberry Street
with you!

Introduction to Assessment

Knowledge: *This level of assessment provides students with an opportunity to recall fundamental facts and information about the story.*

Comprehension: *This level of assessment provides students with an opportunity to demonstrate a basic understanding of the story.*

Application: *This level of assessment provides students with an opportunity to use information about or from the story in a new way.*

Analysis: *This level of assessment provides your students with an opportunity to examine a part of the story or the style of the author carefully in order to better understand it.*

Synthesis: *This level of assessment provides students with an opportunity to put parts from the story together in a new way to form a new idea or product.*

Evaluation: *This level of assessment provides students with an opportunity to form and present an opinion backed up by sound reasoning.*

Knowledge

Here are a few ideas you can adapt to any of Dr. Seuss's books your students have studied.

- Ask student volunteers to draw 2 inch (5 cm) square black line pictures of the main characters in the story. Collect their pictures and use them to construct a test that requires students to match characters' names with their pictures.

- Supply students with a piece of graph paper and ask them to create a wordsearch or crossword puzzle using the characters in the story.

- Extract quotations from the story and ask the students to match the quotations with the characters who said them.

- Prepare, or have the students prepare, pictures of some of the main events in the story. They will then arrange scrambled story pictures in sequential order.

- Prepare sentences that reflect the main ideas or events in the story. Your students will then arrange scrambled story sentences in sequential order.

- Ask students to create a "Wanted Poster" for one of the main characters.

- Provide students with a sheet of drawing paper on which they are to recall details about the setting by creating a picture of where a part of the story took place.

- Ask students to retell the story!

About the Story

Choose one of these task cards and do what the card asks you to do.

Look at this page from the story. In words or pictures, tell what comes just before it.	Turn to page _____. In your own words, tell what the idea on this page means.
Here is a quote from the story. Why was this said?	If there was one more page in this book, what do you think would be on it?
Look at this page from the story. In words or pictures, tell what comes just after it.	What does this story mean to you?
Explain how the main character felt at the beginning, middle, and end of the story.	What is a question you have about this story?

Teacher: Adapt these task cards for specific books.

Design a Lesson Plan

It is now your turn to apply what you know about what your class likes to do when studying a book. Use the Dr. Seuss book, *Green Eggs and Ham.* Design a "lesson plan" for teaching the book to your classmates!

Green Eggs and Ham

by _____

publisher _____

copyright date _____

Summary

_____

_____

_____

Before Reading the Book
idea:

While Reading the Book
idea:

After Reading the Book
idea:

It's now time to teach your lesson. Have fun!

Which Could Be Dr. Seuss?

Which one of these drawings looks most like Dr. Seuss might have done it? Write his name below the drawing you choose. Color the pictures.

108

You're the Author

Read the words written on each of these fish bodies. Choose one of the ideas and do it.

Change something that happens in the story. How would your change make the story different?

Think of three new titles for the story that would give readers a good idea what the story is about.

Pretend you are one of the characters in the story. What would this character say and do if pulled from the page to tell us more?

Think About It

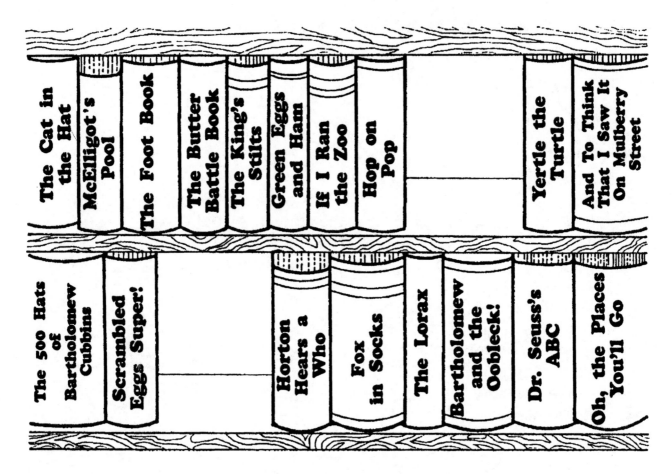

Look at this shelf of books. Choose one or more of the following activities to complete.

- Decide which character is which book you would most like to spend the day with and why.

- Judge whether or not a character should have acted in a particular way.

- Choose the book you like the most and convince us why we should also like this book best.

- Compare two of these books. Discuss ways they are alike and ways they are different.

- Decide if a story really could have happened and justify reasons for your decision.

Bibliography

Other Books by Dr. Seuss

In addition to the books referred to in this publication, Dr. Seuss has written and illustrated a wealth of other books you will want to include in your Dr. Seuss library! Here is a partial listing of his works.

The Cat in the Hat Comes Back (Random House, 1958)

The Cat in the Hat Song Book (Random House, 1967)

Dr. Seuss's Sleep Book (Random House, 1962)

Fox in Socks (Random House, 1965)

Great Day for UP! (Random House, 1974)

Green Eggs and Ham (Random House, 1960)

Happy Birthday to You! (Random House, 1959)

How the Grinch Stole Christmas! (Random House, 1957)

Horton Hatches the Egg (Random House, 1940)

I Am NOT Going to Get up Today! (Random House, 1987)

1 Can Lick 30 Tigers Today! and Other Stories (Random House, 1969)

If I Ran the Circus (Random House, 1956)

McElligot's Pool (Random House, 1947)

Mr. Brown Can Moo! Can You? (Random House, 1970)

On Beyond Zebra! (Random House, 1955)

One Fish Two Fish Red Fish Blue Fish (Random House, 1960)

The Shape of Me and Other Stuff (Random House, 1973)

There's a Wocket in my Pocket! (Random House, 1974)

Thidwick the Big-Hearted Moose (Random House, 1948)

You're Only Old Once! (Random House, 1986)

Books for Alphabet Center

Here is a partial listing of some excellent alphabet books that can be used in the Alphabet Center described on page 34.

Anno, Mitsumasa. *Anno's Alphabet: An Adventure in Imagination*. (Crowell, 1975)

Base, Graeme. *Animalia*. (Harry N. Abrams, 1986)

Elting, Mary and Michael Folsam. *Q is for Duck*. (Clarion, 1980)

Hague, Kathleen. *Alphabears: An ABC Book*. (Holt, Rinehart and Winston, 1984)

Hoban, Tana. *A, B, See!* (Greenwillow, 1982)

Lobel, Arnold and Anita Lobel. *On Market Street*. (Greenwillow, 1981)

Martin, Jr., Bill and John Archambault. *Chicka Chicka Boom Boom*. (Simon & Schuster, 1989)

Musgrove, Margaret. *Ashanti to Zulu*. (Dial, 1980)

Wildsmith, Brian. *Brian Wildsmith Is ABC*. (Watts, 1962)

Bibliography *(cont.)*

Additional Resources

Bernstein, Peter W. "Unforgettable Dr. Seuss," *Reader's Digest*. (April, 1992)

Bernstein, Robert. "A Most Special Privilege," *American Bookseller*. (December, 1991)

Brezzo, S. L. *Dr. Seuss from THEN to NOW*. (Random House, 1986)

Hopkins, Lee Bennett. *Books Are By People*. (Citation Press, 1969)

Moje, Elizabeth B. and Woan-Ru Shyu. "Oh, the places you've taken us: RT's tribute to Dr. Seuss," *The Reading Teacher* (May, 1992)

Sneider, Cary 1. **Oobleck: What Do Scientists Do?** (4-8) (Lawrence Hall of Science, University of California at Berkeley, 1988)

Something About the Author, Volume 28. (Gale Research Company, 1982)

Answer Key

Page 13

Page 33

Page 42

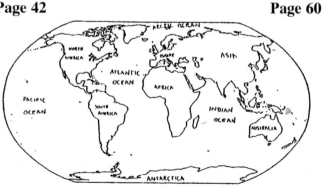

Page 60

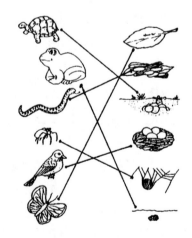

Page 55

1. 90 hats	2. 135 hats	3. 18 hats
4. 192 hats	5. 103 hats	6. 50 hats

Page 71

List 1: sent, spent, tent rent

List 2: scratch, hatch, match, batch

List 3: trick, stick, pick, brick

List 4: land, stand, hand, band

List 5: took, book, hook, shook
